RETURN OF THE LOST TEN TRIBES

AND BUILDING TWO TEMPLES

GLEN W. PARK

RETURN OF THE LOST TEN TRIBES – AND BUILDING TWO TEMPLES

By Glen W. Park

Published by Vision, Inc.
Publications Division
P. O. Box 17181
Salt Lake City, UT 84117

© Copyright 2008-2020 By Glen W. Park, Salt Lake City, Utah. All Rights Reserved. No part of this publication may be used or reproduced in any manner, stored in a retrieval system now known or to be invented, or transmitted in any form or by any means—printed, electronic, digital, photocopy, recording, or any other—except for brief quotations in printed reviews, without the prior written permission of the author.

ISBN: 978-0-9826076-3-3

Library of Congress Control Number: 2020912093.

Cover Design by Glen W. Park

Cover Image: Used by permission of KDP.

Printed in the United States of America

CONTENTS

Chapter 1 Introduction   5
Chapter 2 The Lost Ten Tribes – Separation From The
    Kingdom of Judah   7
Chapter 3 The Lost Ten Tribes and Captive Judah   17
Chapter 4 Continued Killing and Scattering of Israel   22
Chapter 5 Review of The Allegory of The Tame and
    Wild Olive Trees   24
Chapter 6 The Lord Remembers Israel   38
Chapter 7 The Scattering, Then - The Gathering of
    Israel Begins   50
Chapter 8 What Other Part of The House of Israel Plays
    A Role in the Gathering of Israel?   58
Chapter 9 God Continues To Fight Israel's Battles   66
Chapter 10 Two Prophets Fight For Israel   76
Chapter 11 What About The City of Enoch? When and
    To Where Will It Return?   81
Chapter 12 Where Are The Lost Ten Tribes?   86
Chapter 13 Return—Restoration of The Lost Ten Tribes   94
Chapter 14 Synopsis of *The Second Coming and
    The Last Days*   102
Chapter 15 Possible Scenarios: Wars and Plagues
    and Destruction of The Wicked   106
Chapter 16 Temples   128
Chapter 17 Possible Scenarios: Building The Temple
    In Old Jerusalem   137
Chapter 18 Building The Temple In New Jerusalem   142
Chapter 19 Conclusion   146
About The Author   148
Sources Cited   149

GLEN W. PARK

Chapter 1

INTRODUCTION

In my recently-published book *The Second Coming and The Last Days*, I write of numerous events to occur during the last days, principally the few years immediately preceding the second coming of the Lord Jesus Christ.

In this book, we will include only a few of those events, but will focus on: (1) the scattering and casting out of Israel; (2) the gathering of Israel; (2) the restoration of the lost ten tribes of Israel, and (3) the building of two temples of great significance—at Jerusalem, in the Middle East, and in Zion, the New Jerusalem, in the State of Missouri, in the United States.

Many have written about the restoration—or return—of the lost ten tribes of Israel, but there are few subjects about which less complete definitive information is available. Numerous questions remain seemingly unanswered about this interesting and important subject. Moreover, there are many mistaken ideas and interpretations of the facts surrounding where they were "lost," and how and when they will return and where they will go, and what they will do when they return.

Here are a few of these mistaken interpretations held and taught by ministers and members of various religions.

1 - The Old Testament prophet Jeremiah holds the key to the return of the lost ten tribes.

2 - The lost ten tribes were taken from the northern kingdom of Israel into a north country, Assyria. They were all later scattered from there among other nations in the world, period.

3 - The gathering and return of the lost ten tribes will be accomplished by the return to the land—State—of Israel in the Middle East as with the Jewish people.

4 – Related to, but separate from, their restoration, the Jewish belief that before the coming of the Lord, Elijah will hereafter be sent to turn the heart of the fathers to the children, and the heart of the children to the fathers. The Jews and others are still awaiting the future coming of Elijah the prophet. At the meal celebrating the Passover, the Jews place an extra chair for Elijah to sit at the table for the Passover.

Later in this book, we will discuss how and when—or approximately when—these events have occurred or will yet occur.

Chapter 2

THE LOST TEN TRIBES

SEPARATION FROM THE KINGDOM OF JUDAH

According to the Jewish Virtual Library, "[t]he ten lost tribes refers to the legend concerning the fate of the ten tribes constituting the northern Kingdom of Israel."[1]

Note the use of the word "legend", which means a story from the past that is believed by many, but that cannot be proved to be true.

Most, if not all, things in history—even the immediate-past history—are difficult to totally prove. With the ability today to photo shop words, images, even videos, many so-called "facts" can actually be fabrications that appear to be factual, but are not. Even the birth, life, death and resurrection of Jesus Christ may not be legally provable, but for millions, are literally believed. I offer my personal witness, gained through the witness of the Holy Ghost to me and to my spirit, that Jesus Christ is the divine Son of God, the Father. He taught those things His Father commanded Him to teach. He suffered for the sins of all mankind in His great atoning sacrifice. He suffered further on the cross at Calvary, and He gave up His own life so that He could complete the atonement for mankind, and then bring about the resurrection of every mortal who would ever live in this and other worlds.

Some may refer to this, my belief as a legend, but that claim does not, and will never, make that belief any less true or factual.

King David established the united Kingdom of Israel. Following David's death, his son Solomon reigned in his stead. At first, and for many years, during his reign over united Israel, Solomon was obedient to God's commandments. He was even chosen by the Lord to build the magnificent temple at Jerusalem.

Solomon had many wives. Some of them did not believe in the true God. They worshiped idols. As Solomon grew old, his wives wanted him to worship their idols. He chose to do the wrong thing. He offered sacrifices to the idols. This obviously displeased the Lord. He told Solomon that his kingdom would be divided after his death. That is exactly what happened.

Following the death of King Solomon, the son of David, Solomon's son, Rehoboam, reigned in his stead. When Rehoboam unwisely followed the counsel of his young advisers, and promised to increase, rather than lower, taxes on the people, ten of the twelve land tribes of Israel, rebelled and established Jeroboam to be their king. Thus came about the division of the twelve tribes of Israel into two separate kingdoms.

Thus, as stated above, following the reign of King Solomon, the twelve tribes of Israel were, because of iniquity, divided into two parts: the northern Kingdom of Israel, having ten of the tribes; and the southern Kingdom of Judah, which included Judah, part of Simeon that had been absorbed into Judah, part of Benjamin, and the people of the Tribe of Levi, who lived among them of the original Israelite nation. The Tribe of Levi did not have their own land, for it was they who officiated in the temple in Jerusalem. Therefore, it is said that they were not one of the land tribes of Israel. Because the larger part of the tribe of Simeon was included in the northern kingdom, we speak of the southern Kingdom of Judah as having only the tribe of Judah and tribe of Benjamin (with part of Benjamin even being part of the northern Kingdom of Israel.)

RETURN OF THE LOST TEN TRIBES

The lost ten tribes were the greater part of those ten tribes that were conquered and removed from the Kingdom of Israel by the Assyrian Empire at about 722 BC. They include the tribes of Reuben, Simeon, Dan, Naphtali, Gad, Asher, Issachar, Zebulun, Manasseh and Ephraim.

Let us read numerous passages of scripture concerning the ten tribes of Israel, who after a period of time became lost to the world, although not to the Lord.

26 ¶ And Jeroboam the son of Nebat, an Ephrathite of Zereda, Solomon's servant, whose mother's name *was* Zeruah, a widow woman, even he lifted up *his* hand against the king.

27 And this *was* the cause that he lifted up *his* hand against the king: Solomon built Millo, *and* repaired the breaches of the city of David his father.

28 And the man Jeroboam *was* a mighty man of valour: and Solomon seeing the young man that he was industrious, he made him ruler over all the charge of the house of Joseph.

29 And it came to pass at that time **when Jeroboam went out of Jerusalem, that the prophet Ahijah the Shilonite found him in the way; and he had clad himself with a new garment; and** they two *were* alone in the field:

30 And **Ahijah caught the new garment that** *was* **on him, and rent it** *in* **twelve pieces:**

31 **And he said to Jeroboam, Take thee ten pieces: for thus saith the LORD, the God of Israel, Behold, I will rend the kingdom out of the hand of Solomon, and will give ten tribes to thee:**

> 32 (But he shall have one tribe for my servant David's sake, and for Jerusalem's sake, the city which I have chosen out of all the tribes of Israel:)
> 33 Because that they have forsaken me, and have worshipped Ashtoreth the goddess of the Zidonians, Chemosh the god of the Moabites, and Milcom the god of the children of Ammon, and have not walked in my ways, to do *that which is* right in mine eyes, and *to keep* my statutes and my judgments, as *did* David his father.
> 34 Howbeit I will not take the whole kingdom out of his hand: but I will make him prince all the days of his life for David my servant's sake, whom I chose, because he kept my commandments and my statutes:
> 35 But I will take the kingdom out of his son's hand, and will give it unto thee, *even* ten tribes.[2]

As His prophet Ahijah told Jeroboam, the Lord had determined that the children of Israel had been poorly led and gone astray, so the bulk of the kingdom would be given to one other than from the line of David and Solomon.

Just as the Prophet Ahijah had spoken, most of Israel rebelled against Rehoboam, Solomon's son and David's grandson, and followed after Jeroboam, as we can read below:

> 19 So Israel rebelled against the house of David unto this day.
> 20 And it came to pass, when all Israel heard that Jeroboam was come again, that they sent and called him unto the congregation, and made him king over all Israel: there was none that followed the house of David, but the tribe of Judah only.
> 21 ¶ And when Rehoboam was come to Jerusalem, he assembled all the house of Judah, with the tribe of Benjamin, an hundred and fourscore thousand chosen men, which were warriors, to fight

against the house of Israel, to bring the kingdom again to Rehoboam the son of Solomon.

22 But the word of God came unto Shemaiah the man of God, saying,

23 Speak unto Rehoboam, the son of Solomon, king of Judah, and unto all the house of Judah and Benjamin, and to the remnant of the people, saying,

24 Thus saith the LORD, Ye shall not go up, nor fight against your brethren the children of Israel: return every man to his house; for this thing is from me. They hearkened therefore to the word of the LORD, and returned to depart, according to the word of the LORD.[3]

Thus, after the ten tribes had rebelled and left the Kingdom of Judah, rebelling against the reign of Solomon's son, Rehoboam, he was about to send his army to fight against those tribes and force them to return to be under his reign. But the Lord commanded Rehoboam, through the mouth of His prophet, Shemaiah, that he must not go up or fight against the children of Israel. Rehoboam and his warriors obeyed the commandment of the Lord.

Unfortunately, Jeroboam and the northern Kingdom of Israel speedily turned away from following the commandments of the Lord. In the Book of Isaiah, the Lord speaks His displeasure about Israel in two separate chapters as follows:

First, in Isaiah 7:8-9, and then in Chapter 8:4, the Lord speaks His displeasure and warns Israel:

8 For the head of Syria *is* Damascus, and the head of Damascus *is* Rezin; and within threescore and five years shall Ephraim be broken, that it be not a people.

9 And the head of Ephraim *is* Samaria, and the head of Samaria *is* Remaliah's son. If ye will not believe, surely ye shall not be established.[4]

(See also 2 Nephi 17:8.)

> 4 For before the child shall have knowledge to cry, My father, and my mother, the riches of Damascus and the spoil of Samaria shall be taken away before the king of Assyria.[5] (See also 2 Ne 18:4.)

The Lord speaks similar condemnation, while offering mercy for repentance, through the Prophet Jeremiah:

> Go and proclaim these words toward the north, and say, Return, thou backsliding Israel, saith the LORD; *and* I will not cause mine anger to fall upon you: for I *am* merciful, saith the LORD, *and* I will not keep *anger* for ever.[6]

The Lord continues this same line of accusation in I Kings:

> 15 For the LORD shall smite Israel, as a reed is shaken in the water, and he shall root up Israel out of this good land, which he gave to their fathers, and shall scatter them beyond the river, because they have made their **groves**, provoking the LORD to anger.
> 16 And he shall give Israel up because of the sins of Jeroboam, who did sin, and who made Israel to sin.[7]

Because Jeroboam sinned, and led Israel into sin, the Lord announced that He would no longer protect Israel. Although the Lord had freed them from captivity in Egypt, they had squandered His goodwill toward them. The Lord had not forsaken Israel, but they had forsaken Him, and turned to dumb and worthless idols.

The term "groves", in verse 15 above, refers to the heathens' worship of nature and idols. The idol Asherah, was usually placed and worshipped in groves, which places became associated with gross immorality. Due to these and other of Israel's iniquities, God would allow their kingdom to be defeated and carried away into captivity. We can read the Lord's words and their fulfillment:

> 5 ¶ Then the king of Assyria came up throughout all the land, and went up to Samaria, and besieged it three years.
> 6 ¶ In the ninth year of Hoshea the king of Assyria took Samaria, and carried Israel away into Assyria, and placed them in Halah and in Habor *by* the river of Gozan, and in the cities of the Medes.
> 7 For *so* it was, that the children of Israel had sinned against the LORD their God, which had brought them up out of the land of Egypt, from under the hand of Pharaoh king of Egypt, and had feared other gods,
> 8 And walked in the statutes of the heathen, whom the LORD cast out from before the children of Israel, and of the kings of Israel, which they had made.[8]

We can read more of the Lord's punishment, which came about at the hands of the Assyrians, because Israel had sinned and not repented of their wicked ways:

> 18 Therefore the LORD was very angry with Israel, and removed them out of his sight: there was none left but the tribe of Judah only.
> 19 Also Judah kept not the commandments of the LORD their God, but walked in the statutes of Israel which they made.
> 20 And the LORD rejected all the seed of Israel, and afflicted them, and delivered them

into the hand of spoilers, until he had cast them out of his sight.⁹

We can read another account of Israel's defeat and captivity in II *Kings*.

> 9 ¶ And it came to pass in the fourth year of king Hezekiah, which *was* the seventh year of Hoshea son of Elah king of Israel, *that* Shalmaneser king of Assyria came up against Samaria, and besieged it.
> 10 And at the end of three years they took it: *even* in the sixth year of Hezekiah, that *is* the ninth year of Hoshea king of Israel, Samaria was taken.
> 11 And the king of Assyria did carry away Israel unto Assyria, and put them in Halah and in Habor *by* the river of Gozan, and in the cities of the Medes:
> 12 Because they obeyed not the voice of the LORD their God, but transgressed his covenant, *and* all that Moses the servant of the LORD commanded, and would not hear *them,* nor do *them.*[10]

Isaiah teaches us the cause—which we should know after reading the scriptural citations above—for Israel's destruction and captivity:

> 24 Who gave Jacob for a spoil, and Israel to the robbers? did not the LORD, he against whom we have sinned? for they would not walk in his ways, neither were they obedient unto his law.
> 25 Therefore he hath poured upon him the fury of his anger, and the strength of battle: and it hath set him on fire round about, yet he knew not; and it burned him, yet he laid *it* not to heart.[11]

In the above verses, Isaiah teaches that although the Lord's anger was kindled and Israel was set on fire, yet he—the people of Israel—never took it to his—their—heart. In other words, Israel never came to know or learn anything from the consequences of their sins.

Isaiah continues to describe the negative consequences of Israel's disobedience, including people coming from far away:

> 11 And I will make all my mountains a way,
> and my highways shall be exalted.
> 12 Behold, these shall come from far: and, lo, these from the north and from the west; and these from the land of Sinim.[12]

The Lord shall remove the mountains and raise the valleys.

The country referred to in verse 12 is not known. It is only known that it is the most far-distant land known of by the writer, Isaiah. Some even believe it may be China.

So, as stated herein above, the sole reason for which Israel was besieged, conquered and taken captive was their disobedience to the Lord. They would neither "hear" nor "do" what the Lord commanded them, as we have just read in II Kings. Disobedience is never a formula for success or happiness. In fact, it is always a formula for disaster. It certainly was for the Kingdom of Israel.

As stated before, ten tribes made up the northern Kingdom of Israel, which was defeated by the Assyrians. Then they were taken captive into Assyria. Some of them were scattered among many nations, even those far away. The larger portion of them was cast out and taken away from Assyria, as we will read hereinafter.

Prior to the defeat by Assyria of the northern kingdom, the two kingdoms—northern and southern—had fought each other for many years. Both Rehoboam and Jeroboam were wicked kings. Their successors continued their wickedness. The people of both kingdoms followed the wickedness of their respective kings. Both kingdoms, therefore, lost favor in the sight of the Lord.

In this chapter, we have read the prophecies of the division, or separation, of the ten tribes into the northern Kingdom of Israel, from the two (actually 1-1/2) tribes of the southern kingdom, that made up the Kingdom of Judah.

Those prophecies were fulfilled precisely as foretold by the Lord through His prophets.

Chapter 3

THE LOST TEN TRIBES AND CAPTIVE JUDAH

BOTH KINGDOMS SHALL BE DEFEATED AND TAKEN AWAY CAPTIVE

THE KINGDOM OF ISRAEL

The ten tribes of Israel—lived under the reigns of several kings following Jeroboam. These kings, combined, reigned, as the northern Kingdom of Israel endured for two hundred years, beginning when they separated themselves from the Kingdom of Judah in 922 B. C.

In 722 B.C., the Kingdom of Israel was defeated by the Assyrians and, following that defeat, its citizens were exiled—taken captive—to Assyria, as noted above.

Where they went from there is only partially known. They were first taken to Halah, Habor and Hara, and to the river Gozan "unto this day," as is recorded in II Kings 17. Halah is a city in Assyria, in the district of Media—the ancient country or area of modern-day northwestern Iran. Habor, is believed to be on the largest perennial tributary to the Euphrates River in modern-day Syria. Hara is another city or district in ancient Assyria. The Gozan River is believed to be in Afghanistan and/or Central Asia.

"Unto this day" would have been until the time of writing, centuries before the birth of Jesus Christ.

THE KINGDOM OF JUDAH

The Kingdom of Judah was destroyed by the Babylonians in 598-582 B.C. The king of Babylon took the most influential citizens of Judah to Babylon, in approximately 586 B.C.

The Prophet Jeremiah, who was not taken captive, sent word from Jerusalem to the elders who had been carried away captive how long to expect to be in captivity. He instructs the captive Jews to build houses, plant gardens, get married, have children, and have your children marry and have children. The Lord wants them to increase in numbers, and not grow smaller. Seek to live in peace.

The Lord further warns the people of captive Judah to not listen to, nor follow or believe the supposed "prophets" and diviners among them, since they will only deceive them, for the Lord did not send them to the captives. They will prophesy falsely.

> 1 NOW these *are* the words of the letter that Jeremiah the prophet sent from Jerusalem unto the residue of the elders which were carried away captives, and to the priests, and to the prophets, and to all the people whom Nebuchadnezzar had carried away captive from Jerusalem to Babylon;
> 4 Thus saith the LORD of hosts, the God of

> Israel, unto all that are carried away captives, whom I have caused to be carried away from Jerusalem unto Babylon;
>
> 5 Build ye houses, and dwell *in them;* and plant gardens, and eat the fruit of them;
>
> 6 Take ye wives, and beget sons and daughters; and take wives for your sons, and give your daughters to husbands, that they may bear sons and daughters; that ye may be increased there, and not diminished.
>
> 7 And seek the peace of the city whither I have caused you to be carried away captives, and pray unto the LORD for it: for in the peace thereof shall ye have peace.
>
> 8 ¶ For thus saith the LORD of hosts, the God of Israel; Let not your prophets and your diviners, that *be* in the midst of you, deceive you, neither hearken to your dreams which ye cause to be dreamed.
>
> 9 For they prophesy falsely unto you in my name: I have not sent them, saith the LORD.
>
> 10 ¶ For thus saith the LORD, That after seventy years be accomplished at Babylon I will visit you, and perform my good word toward you, in causing you to return to this place.[13]

We have just read that Jeremiah told the captive Jews that they and their children and grandchildren would remain in captivity for seventy (70) years, after which time the Lord would cause them to return to Jerusalem.

The Lord, through Jeremiah, then further instructs captive Judah in Babylon. He tells them that he has thoughts of peace and not evil towards them.

> 11 For I know the thoughts that I think toward you, saith the LORD, thoughts of peace, and not of evil, to give you an expected end.

> 12 Then shall ye call upon me, and ye shall go and pray unto me, and I will hearken unto you.
> 13 And ye shall seek me, and find *me,* when ye shall search for me with all your heart.[14]

In the above verses 11 through 13, the Lord further reassures Judah that He will hear and bless them as they pray to Him. If they seek Him, they will find Him.

Then the Lord, in the next verses, tells captive Judah that He will end their captivity. He will gather them from all nations and from everywhere they have been driven. They shall be brought again to Jerusalem.

Obviously, "they" refers to the descendants of the many captives, for this gathering will not occur until seventy years have passed.

> 14 And I will be found of you, saith the LORD: and I will turn away your captivity, and I will gather you from all the nations, and from all the places whither I have driven you, saith the LORD; and I will bring you again into the place whence I caused you to be carried away captive.
> 15 ¶ Because ye have said, The LORD hath raised us up prophets in Babylon;
> 16 *Know* that thus saith the LORD of the king that sitteth upon the throne of David, and of all the people that dwelleth in this city, *and* of your brethren that are not gone forth with you into captivity;
> 17 Thus saith the LORD of hosts; Behold, I will send upon them the sword, the famine, and the pestilence, and will make them like vile figs, that cannot be eaten, they are so evil.
> 18 And I will persecute them with the sword, with the famine, and with the pestilence, and will deliver them to be removed to all the kingdoms of the

> earth, to be a curse, and an astonishment, and an hissing, and a reproach, among all the nations whither I have driven them:
>
> 19 Because they have not hearkened to my words, saith the LORD, which I sent unto them by my servants the prophets, rising up early and sending *them;* but ye would not hear, saith the LORD.
>
> 20 ¶ Hear ye therefore the word of the LORD, all ye of the captivity, whom I have sent from Jerusalem to Babylon . . .[15]

Note that the Lord speaks forcefully against the "supposed prophets" raised up in Babylon. They are not of Him. And of the people in and about Jerusalem who were not taken captive into Babylon, the Lord declares that they do not hearken to His words.

Therefore, He will send unto them the sword, famine and pestilence. Because they are so evil, the Lord will allow them to be removed and scattered, to all kingdoms—nations—of the earth.

In this chapter, we have read the prophecies of the defeat of both the northern kingdom—ten tribes—and the southern kingdom—two tribes—and of both kingdoms being taken away into captivity. The ten tribes were removed first, in 722 B.C. into Assyria, and then farther, into the north countries.

The Kingdom of Judah was defeated by Babylon at about 586 B.C., and taken captive into Babylon, there to serve for seventy (70) years.

The next chapters will continue to follow these two separate kingdoms and what is prophesied to happen to them during and after many centuries.

Chapter 4

CONTINUED KILLING AND SCATTERING OF JUDAH

Centuries passed following the defeat and captivity of both of the kingdoms of the children of Israel.

Roman general Pompey conquered Jerusalem and the surrounding areas inhabited by the Jews in 63 B.C. In the decades that followed, thousands of Jews were imprisoned, tortured and crucified before Jesus Christ was born. Many more died in battle. Thousands of others were sold into slavery. Those who were the fittest were forced to become gladiators, who were caused to fight in arenas throughout the Roman Empire.

General Pompey had conquered Syria the year before capturing Judea, which is what the area in and around Jerusalem was then called. Having these two areas as bases for the Roman legions was a significant, strategic accomplishment.

Because the Roman Empire was overextended, being so far from Rome, it treated Judea quite leniently at first. Because the Roman design was to extend its rule into Gallia—present-day France, Belgium, Luxembourg, Parts of Switzerland, Northern Italy, Netherlands and German; Britannia—roughly current-day Scotland; and Germania—other parts of Germany, and to other places nearer to Rome, it needed to build new roads to transport its legions of soldiers needed. Ports also needed to be upgraded. So as time passed, Rome became more and more heavy handed in dealing with the Jews.

From time to time, Judea rebelled. In 4 B.C., a messianic revolt was crushed, and some 2,000 rebellious Jews were crucified.

Life became continually harder for the Jews until the war between the Jews and their Roman rulers from 66 to 70 A.D. Many of the rebels were captured and crucified.

It is thought that during the 100 years between 36 A.D and 135 A.D., millions of Jews were killed in a certain type of genocide.

Following that period, Rome exiled the Jews from their ancestral lands. During the centuries that followed, Christian teachings were consistently critical of Jews. This served, at least in part, in justifying the continuing prejudice and genocide committed against the Jewish people.

Chapter 5

REVIEW OF THE ALLEGORY OF THE TAME AND WILD OLIVE TREES

Chapters 2 and 3 explained much about the defeat, destruction and removal into captivity of both the southern Kingdom of Judah—two of the twelve tribes—and the northern Kingdom of Israel—the ten tribes of the twelve tribes—of Israel.

Having that understanding, it will now be easier than ever before to gain greater understanding of how the Lord, through two (2) prophets, taught us how these scatterings fit into the Lord's plan of salvation and redemption for His people, Israel.

An ancient prophet, Zenos, taught an allegory of tame and wild olive trees. Zenos is quoted by the prophet Jacob—brother of Nephi—in the Book of Jacob in the Book of Mormon. Although not the longest, this is one of the long chapters in all of scripture. We will not review every verse, but will review the most relevant and informative verses from Jacob Chapter 5, to gain additional understanding, or to be a reminder for those who already have that knowledge. We will now proceed with this allegory.

This story relates the account of a man who took a tame olive tree and nourished it in his vineyard. Zenos likens this tame olive tree to Israel, and his entire vineyard to the world and what would come to them.

Throughout this chapter, I will write the word "SUMMARY" after which I will briefly summarize the events of the verse or verses of the allegory. The relevant verse or verses will then follow.

Following the citation of the verse or verses, I will write the words "ACTUAL HISTORY', after which I will briefly tell what actually happened in the history of the tribes of Judah and/or Israel.

Let us put things into proper perspective. Although Jacob writes in approximately 544 B.C., he quotes the Prophet Zenos, who had lived prior to 725 B.C.—perhaps some amount of time before that. How can we know this? Zenos writes of the future scattering of Israel, which history shows—as we have already reviewed herein—began in 722 B.C., when the Assyrians defeated the northern kingdom of Israel, and carried the bulk of the citizens captive into Assyria and, eventually, beyond.

Now, the history of Israel began much earlier, of course. Literally, the story of the Children of Israel, could not start until Jacob—renamed Israel by the Lord—had his twelve children. So, the history of strictly the Children of Israel began before 1900 B.C.

Therefore, this man's vineyard, and therefore, Israel's children's beginnings continued for some 1,178 plus years before their scattering began in 722 B. C.

Before beginning the allegory, we will review the cast of characters in this story. We do not want to do this review at the end, as when the credits come as occurs after the conclusion of a movie. I want us to know who is who before we continue:

Master/Owner/Lord of the vineyard = God the Father;
Vineyard = the world;
One (first servant) = Jesus Christ;
Original olive tree = Israel;

Tame = righteous, obedient;
Wild = unrighteous, disobedient;
Fruit = individual children of Father in Heaven;
Laying up, or preserving fruit" unto mine own self = having an individual child of God saved in the Kingdom of Heaven.
Other servants = Members, and particularly, missionaries of The Church of Jesus Christ of Latter-day Saints.

We will now begin Zenos' allegory.

SUMMARY: The house of Israel is a tame olive tree that a man cared for in his vineyard. As it grew old, it started to go bad, or rotten.

> For behold, thus saith the Lord, I will liken thee, O house of Israel, like unto a tame olive-tree, which a man took and nourished in his vineyard; and it grew, and waxed old, and began to decay.[16]

ACTUAL HISTORY: The children of Israel, after having experienced years of miracles of deliverance, being led and fed, being guided to a land of promise for them, with the Lord fighting their battles for them, turned away from the true God.

Let us see what the master of the vineyard did next.

SUMMARY: Although part of the olive tree put forth tender branches, the top of the tree started to rot. The master directed his servant to trim off the bad branches. Plus, the master had his servant go get branches from a wild olive tree.

> And it came to pass that after many days it began to put forth somewhat a little, young and tender branches; but behold, the main top thereof began to perish.
> And it came to pass that the master of the vineyard saw it, and he said unto his servant: It grieveth me that I should lose this

> tree; wherefore, go and pluck the branches
> from a wild olive-tree, and bring them hither
> unto me; and we will pluck off those main
> branches which are beginning to wither away,
> and we will cast them into the fire that they
> may be burned.[17]

ACTUAL HISTORY: With the main top— leadership of the House of Israel—becoming wicked and rotten from within, the Lord allows many to be killed. Then people from outside Israel come to dwell in the land.

SUMMARY: Now comes one of the important parts of the story. The master took many of the young and tender branches and grafted them "whithersoever I will." We will read that in verse 8.

> And behold, saith the Lord of the
> vineyard, I take away many of these young and
> tender branches, and I will graft them
> whithersoever I will; and it mattereth not that if it
> so be that the root of this tree will perish, I may
> preserve the fruit thereof unto myself; wherefore,
> I will take these young and tender branches, and I
> will graft them whithersoever I will.[18]

ACTUAL HISTORY: The Lord took some of the young and good of the House of Israel "whithersoever [He] will[ed]", which was in "the nethermost part" of the world. Remember some young and good of Judah—the young Daniel, whose dream and his revealing and interpretation of King Nebuchadnezzar's dream, came to Daniel, because of his personal righteousness. Likewise, remember Shadrach, Meshach and Abednego were three young Hebrew men who were thrown into a fiery furnace because they refused to worship the king's image. Their personal righteousness resulted in their not being burned.

SUMMARY: God knows what He wants and what He is doing. It does not matter if we think it is a good idea or not. He knows, and He sees the end from the beginning. We read next that the Lord of the vineyard went to the deepest—farthest—parts of the vineyard and grafted in some of the natural branches of the original, tame olive tree.

> And it came to pass that the Lord of the vineyard went his way, and hid the natural branches of the tame olive-tree in the nethermost parts of the vineyard, some in one and some in another, according to his will and pleasure.[19]

ACTUAL HISTORY: After some 1,178 years o decaying, Israel had turned from the Lord and His commandments and followed after—worshiped—other gods. Then, in 722 B.C., the northern kingdom was defeated—destroyed—and taken captive by the Assyrians.

Then, Judah, the southern kingdom, is destroyed and taken away captive by the Babylonians in 586 B.C.

So, both kingdoms have been literally "cut off", removed and taken from Canaan. Both were taken to the nethermost—deepest, or farthest—parts of the world. They were then in the **poorest spot in the world.** This poorest spot would be where the true gospel of the Lord would not be taught or practiced. Instead, pagan worship of idols was that to which they were exposed.

SUMMARY: The allegory continues. The servant asks why the branches from the tame olive tree had been taken to the farthest part of the world, which had the poorest ground.

> 21 And it came to pass that the servant said unto his master: How comest thou hither to plant this tree, or this branch of the tree? For behold, it was the poorest spot in all the land of thy vineyard.[20]

ACTUAL HISTORY: This farthest, poorest, spot was to where the first and smaller part of the ten tribes, and the southern kingdom of Judah were taken. In time, they both were scattered from their respective places of captivity to be among the nations of the world.

SUMMARY: The next several paragraphs describe where the larger part of the ten tribes was taken.

The Master explains that he went farther still to a "spot of ground [that] was poorer than the first."

> And it came to pass that the Lord of the vineyard said unto his servant: Look hither; behold I have planted another branch of the tree also; and **thou knowest that this spot of ground was poorer than the first**. But, behold the tree. I have nourished it this long time, and it hath brought forth much fruit; therefore, gather it, and lay it up against the season, that I may preserve it unto mine own self.[21]

ACTUAL HISTORY: We need to again consider this matter in the actual history of the House of Israel. If parts of both kingdoms were taken to the farthest place **in** the world, that is also the poorest spot **in** the world, where and how can another place be farther and poorer than that first spot?

Obviously, the answer has these two parts: Farther can only be away from this world. A spot that is poorer than the poorest on Earth must also be somewhere other than on the earth.

Let us think of a place that would be poorer—with less good ground—than this earth. In spiritual terms, it would be a place where The Church of Jesus Christ would not be established or restored. Such a place would not have, at least for a very long time, the opportunity to hear, learn of, or accept the true principles and ordinances of the Lord Jesus Christ's Church. That would be worse, or poorer, than the poorest part of the earth.

To clarify, I will repeat the above explanation in different words. The smaller part of the northern kingdom—that of the ten tribes, was scattered, along with Judah, to the poorest land in the entire world (vineyard.) But the next spot—hither—was poorer than the first.

Note: How can a place be poorer than the poorest spot in the vineyard?

It is not possible **in** the vineyard. It is only possible **outside** of the vineyard.

Let us try the prior three sentences, substituting "world" for "vineyard".

How can a place be poorer than the poorest spot in the world?

It is not possible in the world.

IT IS ONLY POSSIBLE OUTSIDE OF THE WORLD.

That, in fact, is where the lost ten tribes were taken—outside of this world. Later in this book, we will read statements made by modern-day prophets and apostles who will explain more of where they were taken.

SUMMARY: We will now proceed to the third grafting, or planting, of branches/trees in the vineyard. This is of another tree of the vineyard. This is planted in a "good spot." Moreover, the Lord of the vineyard nourishes the tree for a long time. Part of the tree produces good—tame—fruit. The other part produces wild—bad—fruit.

> And he said unto the servant: Look hither and behold the last. Behold, this have I planted in a good spot of ground; and I have nourished it this long time, and only a part of

> the tree hath brought forth tame fruit, and
> the other part of the tree hath brought forth
> wild fruit; behold, I have nourished this tree
> like unto the others.[22]

ACTUAL HISTORY: The third planting of a tree—separation of a part of Israel—was in a good spot of ground. This separation was of the families of Lehi and Ishmael, from Jerusalem, in 600 B.C., who then sailed to the western hemisphere—the Americas.

The above verse also states ". . . only a part of the tree hath brought forth tame fruit—the Nephites for most of their history, (although there were some times when the Lamanites were more righteous than the Nephites)—and the other part of the tree hath brought forth wild fruit—the Lamanites, who were generally wicked.

SUMMARY: After much time had passed, before the end of the life of the vineyard would come, the Lord of the vineyard wanted to try to obtain much more good fruit.

> And it came to pass that a long time had
> passed away, and the Lord of the vineyard said
> unto his servant: Come, let us go down into the
> vineyard, that we may labor again in the
> vineyard. For behold, the time draweth near,
> and the end soon cometh; wherefore, I must lay
> up fruit against the season, unto mine own self.[23]

ACTUAL HISTORY: A long time into the life of the world—in fact, not long before the end of the world—the Lord wanted to help many more come unto eternal life. So, the Master went into the world, Himself. He and Jesus Christ, His Son, personally appeared to Joseph Smith.

SUMMARY: After some time, with good roots, a tree began to produce wild, or bad, fruit. Said the Master of the vineyard:

> Nevertheless, I know that the roots are

> good, and for mine own purpose I have preserved
> them; and because of their much strength they
> have hitherto brought forth, from the wild
> branches, good fruit.[24]

ACTUAL HISTORY: In the world, there would be more than one tree—nation--with good roots. The blood of Israel was spread to all nations of the world. Nonetheless, all the trees of the vineyard eventually were producing wild, bad, fruit—despite having good roots. Let us read why.

SUMMARY: The servant suggested that the reason the trees with good roots were producing bad fruit was the "loftiness of the vineyard." The branches had overcome the good roots, which could then not adequately nourish the branches.

> And it came to pass that the servant
> said unto his master: Is it not the loftiness of
> thy vineyard—have not the branches thereof
> overcome the roots which are good? And
> because the branches have overcome the roots
> thereof, behold they grew faster than the
> strength of the roots, taking strength unto themselves.
> Behold, I say, is not this the cause that the trees of
> thy vineyard have become corrupted?[25]

ACTUAL HISTORY: The loftiness of the branches is a metaphor for the pride, selfishness and haughtiness of the people of the world—both those of the House of Israel and those not of the House of Israel. Those faults in character and that unrighteousness were the actual cause of the wickedness and evil that spread through Israel and other parts of the world.

SUMMARY: So, the Lord decided to bring the scattered branches back to their home, as we will next read.

> And, behold, the roots of the natural branches
> of the tree which I planted whithersoever I would

> are yet alive; wherefore, that I may preserve them also for mine own purpose, I will take of the branches of this tree, and I will graft them in unto them. Yea, I will graft in unto them the branches of their mother tree, that I may preserve the roots also unto mine own self, that when they shall be sufficiently strong perhaps they may bring forth good fruit unto me, and I may yet have glory in the fruit of my vineyard.
>
> And it came to pass that they took from the natural tree which had become wild, and grafted in unto the natural trees, which also had become wild.
>
> And they also took of the natural trees which had become wild, and grafted into their mother tree.[26]

ACTUAL HISTORY: These verses metaphorically describe the gathering and the return of Israel to their homeland—the Land of Canaan—the modern-day State of Israel.

SUMMARY: What follows? We see in verses 58 and 59. After Israel was gathered, there was still much to do. Israel needed to be nourished, the rotten parts be cast into the fire, so the good can overcome the evil branches.

> And we will nourish again the trees of the vineyard, and we will trim up the branches thereof; and we will pluck from the trees those branches which are ripened, that must perish, and cast them into the fire.
>
> And this I do that, perhaps, the roots thereof may take strength because of their goodness; and because of the change of the branches, that the good may overcome the evil.[27]

ACTUAL HISTORY: Nourishing Israel can include several actions: 1 – Fighting their battles; 2 – prospering them; 3 – teaching them the true gospel of Jesus Christ and His commandments; and 4 – ultimately saving them—physically and spiritually.

To ultimately be saved and be with our Father, they must accept and obey the Lord's commandments. This is how they can produce good fruit that is preserved—to obtain eternal life with God our Father.

SUMMARY: The Master of the vineyard wants additional servants to labor diligently in the vineyard to produce more good fruit.

> Wherefore, go to, and call servants, that we may labor diligently with our might in the vineyard, that we may prepare the way, that I may bring forth again the natural fruit, which natural fruit is good and the most precious above all other fruit.[28]

ACTUAL HISTORY: In the latter days, The Church of Jesus Christ of Latter-day Saints was restored to the earth. Right from the start, servants—missionaries—were sent out into many parts of the world to help "prepare the way" for the second coming of the Lord, and to teach true principles to help the people of the world to live righteously in order to reap the blessings of eternal life. This work continues.

SUMMARY: In more than one place in the scriptures, the phrases we will read in the next verse are found. The Master directs his servants to graft in the branches so the last of the trees may be first, and that the first of the trees may be last. They all should be nourished one more time before the end. The natural branches shall be grafted into the natural tree, and they shall bring forth fruit and be one.

> Graft in the branches; begin at the last that they may be first, and that the first may be last, and dig about the trees, both old and

> young, the first and the last; and the last and
> the first, that all may be nourished once again
> for the last time.
> And the branches of the natural tree
> will I graft into the natural branches of the
> tree; and thus will I bring them together again,
> that they shall bring forth the natural fruit,
> and they shall be one.[29]

ACTUAL HISTORY: The Jewish people were the first to have the opportunity to see, hear and accept the Lord Jesus Christ and His gospel and commandments. Most of them chose to reject Him.

Later, the Gentiles were given the opportunity to hear and accept Christ's gospel and commandments—although not in His physical presence. Some—certainly not even close to all—accepted him and chose to obey His commandments.

Thus, the last to get to hear—the Gentiles—were the first to accept and receive the blessings attendant to that. Scattered Israel—the first to get to hear—shall be the last to accept Him, and therefore, the last to receive the attendant blessings.

But eventually, those who accept Christ, the Redeemer, shall be one in the blessings they will receive.

SUMMARY: The vineyard, having been worked with and nourished this last time, produced good fruit. It was no more corrupt. Much good fruit was preserved. Those servants who had helped the master were blessed for their diligence. The bad is cast away and the Lord has joy in his vineyard.

> And it came to pass that when the Lord
> of the vineyard saw that his fruit was good, and that his
> vineyard was no more corrupt, he called up his servants,
> and said unto them: Behold, for this last time have we
> nourished my vineyard; and thou beholdest that I have

> done according to my will; and I have preserved the natural fruit, that it is good, even like as it was in the beginning. And blessed art thou; for because ye have been diligent in laboring with me in my vineyard, and have kept my commandments, and have brought unto me again the natural fruit, that my vineyard is no more corrupted, and the bad is cast away, behold ye shall have joy with me because of the fruit of my vineyard.[30]

ACTUAL HISTORY—Some of this is still to come: Israel will be both gathered and restored from its places where it was scattered and cast out. Most will be brought to the knowledge and testimony of the Redeemer at and following the second coming of the Lord Jesus Christ.

Those servants who have assisted the Lord, with their might, in teaching and leading Israel to the Lord shall be blessed.

SUMMARY: In time, evil fruit shall again come. The master shall gather the good and preserve it unto himself. He will also gather the bad and cast it into its own place. Then the vineyard will be burned.

> And when the time cometh that evil fruit shall again come into my vineyard, then will I cause the good and the bad to be gathered; and the good will I preserve unto myself, and the bad will I cast away into its own place. And then cometh the season and the end; and my vineyard will I cause to be burned with fire.[31]

ACTUAL HISTORY—All of which is still to come: At the end of the Millenium—nearly a thousand years following the second coming of Jesus Christ—there shall be evil once again come to the earth. Satan will thus be loosed one last time. He will lead his evil forces in one last battle against Jesus Christ and His forces of the righteous. Satan, and all who chose to follow him, shall be defeated and cast into their own place—Perdition for Satan and those who followed him in the pre-existence, and some others who later chose to follow him. Others still, shall be cast into the dregs of the lowest of the kingdoms.

Thus concludes the allegory of the tame and wild olive trees. Having read of the scattering of the House of Israel, this allegory and its explanation should have been much clearer, as well as, the application of the allegory to both history and the future of Israel.

Chapter 6

THE LORD REMEMBERS ISRAEL

The Lord has never forgotten Israel—here meaning all of the twelve tribes of Israel. They rejected the Lord and His commandments and they followed after idols and other gods, even centuries before Jesus Christ came to the earth. Therefore, the Lord took away from them His Spirit and much of His protection against their enemies.

This withdrawal by the Lord served two important purposes. Firstly, it was the natural and prophesied consequence of their wickedness. The scriptures repeatedly state that if we keep His commandments and worship Him, the Only True God, we will prosper in the land. If we cease obeying and reverencing Him, we shall be cast out from His presence. Such was the case with both kingdoms of the twelve tribes of Israel.

Secondly, although virtually all of Israel was wicked and had ceased following the Lord's commandments, they were, and are, the chosen people of the Lord.

There is an important and justified reason for this. Our everlasting status with the Lord is not determined solely by our mortal lives on earth. We dwelled in the presence of our Father in Heaven—Elohim—and His Son, Jehovah—He who would create this and other worlds and later come to Earth as Jesus Christ, the Messiah. This pre-Earth existence—the pre-existence—lasted far longer than do our mortal lives. Even the long lives of the patriarchs—some living well over nine hundred years—is exceedingly short in comparison to the length of our pre-existence!

It was in the pre-mortal existence that the people who would become the children of Israel—originally named Jacob—first, and enduringly, showed Father in Heaven that they were more valiant in following His laws and commandments than most others.

Undoubtedly, those who would be the Gentiles and others who on Earth would embrace the Gospel of Jesus Christ with all of their hearts, were also valiant in the pre-existence. Those who did, whose actual bloodline does not run back to one or more of the tribes of Israel, have been adopted into the House of Israel through their baptism into The Church of Jesus Christ of Latter-day Saints.

But as an immense multitude, those originally in the House of Israel were the ones the Lord knew would serve as a leaven to and for all the nations of the world. Leaven, as you know, is used to make dough rise.

Likewise, the House of Israel, scattered throughout the earth, would serve to help, or make, rise—expand and improve—all nations. Ultimately, after the time of the Gentiles has ended, the Gospel of Jesus Christ would be accepted by most of those in the world who have the blood of Israel in their veins.

The Lord spoke to the Prophet Nephi, in the New World, more than five hundred years before the birth of Jesus Christ, of the Lord remembering scattered Israel, as well as, the descendants of Joseph—who are a separate part of the House of Israel.

> For behold, the Lord God has led away from time to time from the house of Israel, according to his

> will and pleasure. And now behold, the Lord
> remembereth all them who have been broken off,
> wherefore he remembereth us also.[32]

In preparation for the events of gathering and restoring that would occur in the latter days, the Lord first restored His gospel and church upon the earth. The Church of Jesus Christ of Latter-day Saints was established—restored—on April 6, 1830, through the Prophet Joseph Smith. That was preceded by the restoration of the Aaronic and Melchisedek Priesthoods. Thereafter, the committing, or bestowal, of the various "keys" needed for the furthering of the work of the Lord took place.

Let us now discuss the appearance of the Prophet Moses in the Kirtland Temple in April 1836. In fact, we will deal with the purpose of his appearance here, as well as, later in this book. The account of his appearance in that temple is as follows:

> 11 After this vision closed, the heavens were gain opened unto us; and Moses appeared before us, and committed unto us **the keys of the gathering of Israel from the four parts of the earth, and the leading of the ten tribes from the land of the north.**[33]

Let us review only the first part of the keys Moses committed: "of the gathering of Israel from the four parts of the earth."

As part of that gathering of Israel, in 1841, Elder Orson Hyde, an Apostle of The Church of Jesus Christ of Latter-day Saints traveled to the Holy Land—more than one hundred years before the State of Israel was created by the United Nations, to dedicate that land for the return of the Jewish people. I will now quote part of his dedicatory prayer:

> [I] dedicate and consecrate this land
> unto Thee, **FOR THE GATHERING TOGETHER OF**

JUDAH'S SCATTERED REMNANTS, according to the predictions of the holy Prophets. ... **INCLINE THEM** to gather in upon this land according to Thy word. Let them come like clouds and like doves to their windows. Let the large ships of the nations bring them from the distant isles; and let kings become their nursing fathers, and queens with motherly fondness wipe the tear of sorrow from their eyes.[34]
(Emphasis added.)

The Prophet Zechariah, in two separate chapters, foretold:

And the Lord shall inherit Judah his portion in the holy land, and shall choose Jerusalem again.[35]

... and Jerusalem shall be inhabited again in her own place, even in Jerusalem.[36]

For more than 1900 years, the orthodox Jews concluded their prayers with the petition, "Next year in Jerusalem." In 1967, 126 years after Elder Hyde's dedicatory prayer, the Jewish people had their dream and petition realized. Back in 1841, only a few thousand Jews lived in the whole land of Palestine. As of 2018, there were just under nine million living in the modern State of Israel!

Although the full gathering of Israel has not occurred, there has been amazing progress in that regard since Elder Hyde's exercise of the keys committed by Moses to the leadership of The Church of Jesus Christ of Latter-day Saints.

When the Savior appeared to the Nephites, again following His resurrection, he stated:

And it shall come to pass that the time cometh, when the fulness of my gospel shall be preached unto them;
And they shall believe in me, that I am

Jesus Christ, the Son of God, and shall pray unto the Father in my name.[37]

In 1855, the Apostle Wilford Woodruff stated:

> The Prophet Isaiah has also prophesied concerning the gathering of Israel in the last days. Note: For there to be a gathering, there must be one or more places to which the gathering could take place.
>
> And it shall come to pass in the last days, that the mountain of the Lord's house shall be established in the top of the mountains, and shall be exalted above the hills; and all nations shall flow unto it.
> And many people shall go and say, Come ye, and let us go up to the mountain of the Lord, to the house of the God of Jacob; and he will teach us of his ways, and we will walk in his paths: for out of Zion shall go forth the law, and the word of the Lord from Jerusalem.[38] (See also The Doctrine and Covenants, Section 133.)

Notice that Isaiah speaks of two separate places—"out of Zion shall go forth the law," plus, "and the word of the Lord from Jerusalem."

The prophet and Church President Joseph F. Smith spoke of these two places to which the gathering would occur:

> Jerusalem of old, after the Jews have been cleansed and sanctified from all their sin, shall become a holy city where the Lord shall dwell and from whence he shall send forth his word unto all people. Likewise, on this continent, the city of Zion, New Jerusalem—shall be built, and from it the law of God shall also go forth. There will be no conflict, for each city shall be headquarters for the Redeemer of the world, and from

> each he shall send forth his proclamations as occasion may require. Jerusalem shall be the gathering place of Judah and his fellows of the house of Israel, and Zion shall be the gathering place of Ephraim and his fellows, upon whose heads shall be conferred 'the richer blessings.' [39]

There are basically four (4) separate groups of the House of Israel: 1 - the Jews, some of whom have been gathered to the State of Israel, and the rest of whom are scattered in other nations. They come from the tribes of Judah and approximately one-half of Benjamin; 2 – the seed, or descendants, of the Nephites and Lamanites—or in other words—the posterity of Lehi, of whom the Book of Mormon gives a history. They can also be referred to as the seed of Joseph—he who was sold into Egypt; 3 – the ten tribes of Israel who are basically some of the various ten tribes captured by the Assyrians and scattered among the people of the whole earth; and 4 - the larger part of the ten tribes of Israel taken captive by the Assyrians, who were driven—cast out—into a land to the north.

Jeremiah 16:10-12 teaches that because the fathers of Israel had forsaken Him, and those who followed had done worse—they all walk after the imagination of their evil heart, so they do not hearken unto Him:

> 10 ¶ And it shall come to pass, when thou shalt shew this people all these words, and they shall say unto thee, Wherefore hath the LORD pronounced all this great evil against us? or what *is* our iniquity? or what *is* our sin that we have committed against the LORD our God?
> 11 Then shalt thou say unto them, Because your fathers have forsaken me, saith the LORD, and have walked after other gods, and have served them, and have worshipped them, and have forsaken me, and have not kept my law;

> 12 And ye have done worse than your fathers; for, behold, ye walk every one after the imagination of his evil heart, that they may not hearken unto me:[40]

Verses 13 through 16 continue the Lord's prophecy of what He will cause to happen, including in the last days.

> 13 Therefore will I cast you out of this land into a land that ye know not, *neither* ye nor your fathers; and there shall ye serve other gods day and night; where I will not shew you favour.
> 14 ¶ Therefore, behold, the days come, saith the LORD, that it shall no more be said, The LORD liveth, that brought up the children of Israel out of the land of Egypt;
> 15 But, The LORD liveth, that brought up the children of Israel from the land of the north, and from all the lands whither he had driven them: and I will bring them again into their land that I gave unto their fathers.
> 16 ¶ Behold, I will send for many fishers, saith the LORD, and they shall fish them; and after will I send for many hunters, and they shall hunt them from every mountain, and from every hill, and out of the holes of the rocks.[41]

Earlier in this book, we read verses 13 and 14, but I here quote them once again, with the two verses that follow them. In verse 13, Jeremiah says the Lord will cast Israel out of their land into a land that they do not know, and there shall they serve other gods day and night—which was not pleasing to the Lord, but being there, Israel would only be given the chance to serve those other gods.

Verse 14 is significant. It teaches that the time will come when the fact that the Lord delivered the children of Israel up out of the land of Egypt, through the Dead Sea on dry ground, then causing that sea to close upon, and drown, the chariot army of Egypt, thereby saving Israel from certain death—then feeding Israel for forty years—all of those doings of the Lord—shall hereafter not be the significant thing the children of Israel would remember and emphasize, for what was to come would be much more remarkable.

Verse 15 completes the thought from verse 14: Instead, it shall be said that He brought the children of Israel, both by gathering Judah, and more especially, by bringing the lost ten tribes from the land of the north, and from all the lands where they had been taken, and that He brought them again into their land that He had given their fathers.

Verse 16, in my mind, speaks of two separate ways—even events—by which the Lord would bring back Israel. He would send many fishers. Jesus Christ called His disciples to be "fishers of men." They would preach to men, one by one., or one small group by one small group. That method would "gather" individuals from amongst the nations of the world.

Thereafter, the Lord would send hunters to find the multitude of Israel—the lost ten tribes—from every mountain, hill and hole in the rocks of the place to which they had been taken.

These verses tell us that what the Lord will do for the children of Israel shall be so much more spectacular than the wondrous things He did in bringing their fathers out of Egypt.

Remember, that deliverance from Egypt includes wonders and miracles: the Passover of the Destroying Angel; making the Dead Sea open up for their fathers to cross it on dry land; closing the waters on Pharoah's army of chariots, killing them and thereby saving Israel; providing manna, and quail; leading them by a cloud during the day and by a pillar of fire at night. All of these shall be much less remarkable when compared with what will happen hereafter when the Lord gathers Israel and restores the lost ten tribes!

Because the above prophecy was delivered from the Lord through the prophet Jeremiah, some religious leaders mistakenly believe that Jeremiah holds the keys to the lost ten tribes. The truth is that the prophet Moses held those keys, until he delivered them to Joseph Smith and Oliver Cowdery.

The account is related in The Doctrine and Covenants. This Section speaks of visions of the Savior and of several prophets that occurred on the anniversary of the Passover in Egypt, on April 3, 1836 in the newly-dedicated Kirtland Temple, in Kirtland, Ohio. I will quote again the short account of the appearance of Moses. After the Savior had appeared, then the Prophet Moses appeared:

> After this vision closed, the heavens were again opened unto us; and Moses appeared before us, and committed unto us the keys of the gathering of Israel from the four parts of the earth, and the leading of the ten tribes from the land of the north.[42]

Note that the keys Moses gave to the Prophet Joseph Smith and Oliver Cowdery were for **two (2) distinct matters—"the gathering of Israel from the four parts of the earth;"** and **"the leading of the ten tribes from the land of the north."**

This combination of the return of Israel is further spoken of in the tenth Article of Faith of The Church of Jesus Christ of Latter-day Saints, which reads in pertinent part:

> We believe in the literal gathering of Israel and in the restoration of the Ten Tribes; . . .[43]

We see that the key to both the gathering of Israel from the four parts of the earth **AND** the restoration of the ten tribes, were bestowed upon Joseph Smith and Oliver Cowdery. Let us dissect this.

The gathering of Israel is "from the four parts of the earth." That would mean that the gathering would be from every part and corner of the earth. Therefore, parts of Israel are gathered, piece-by-piece, as it were. This is necessary because the Lord caused that the descendants of the twelve tribes of Israel were dispersed—scattered—among all of the nations of the earth. They were to serve as the leaven among the nations that would eventually serve to raise themselves and others with faith, having the chosen blood of Israel spread throughout the world. This leavening would later prove a blessing for all of the peoples of the earth.

But the "restoration of the ten tribes" means something distinct and different, in at least two ways.

First, to restore, means that it is altogether brought back in its entirety; and

Second, since the gathering "collects" parts and pieces of Israel from every place in the earth, the restoration of a larger segment of Israel would need to come from somewhere else, not currently spread throughout various parts of the earth. In the chapters to follow, we will work to determine where, or basically where, they are and from where they will come, how they will return, and what they will do when they are restored.

Even Nephi, in the Book of Mormon, spoke of the lost tribes—even the "more part of all the tribes"—having been led away, as well as of the then-coming scattering of the house of Israel. Subsequent to that scattering, Nephi speaks of "a mighty nation among the Gentiles—which nation is the United States of America—upon which the Lord would do—and has done—a marvelous work among the Gentiles. This work shall lead to great blessings not only upon the Gentiles, but also unto the House of Israel, and indeed, the rest of the world:

> 3 Wherefore, the things of which I have read are things pertaining to things both temporal and spiritual; for it appears that the house of Israel, sooner or later, will be scattered upon all the face of the earth, and also among all nations.

4 And behold, there are many who are already lost from the knowledge of those who are at Jerusalem. Yea, the more part of all the tribes have been led away; and they are scattered to and fro upon the isles of the sea; and whither they are none of us knoweth, save that we know that they have been led away.

5 And since they have been led away, these things have been prophesied concerning them, and also concerning all those who shall hereafter be scattered and be confounded, because of the Holy One of Israel; for against him will they harden their hearts; wherefore, they shall be scattered among all nations and shall be hated of all men.

6 Nevertheless, after they shall be nursed by the Gentiles, and the Lord has lifted up his hand upon the Gentiles and set them up for a standard, and their children have been carried in their arms, and their daughters have been carried upon their shoulders, behold these things of which are spoken are temporal; for thus are the covenants of the Lord with our fathers; and it meaneth us in the days to come, and also all our brethren who are of the house of Israel.

7 And it meaneth that the time cometh that after all the house of Israel have been scattered and confounded, that the Lord God will raise up a mighty nation among the Gentiles, yea, even upon the face of this land; and by them shall our seed be scattered.

8 And after our seed is scattered the Lord God will proceed to do a marvelous work among the Gentiles, which shall be of great worth unto our seed; wherefore, it is likened unto their being nourished by the Gentiles and being carried in their arms and upon their shoulders.

9 And it shall also be of worth unto the Gentiles; and not only unto the Gentiles but unto

all the house of Israel, unto the making known
of the covenants of the Father of heaven unto
Abraham, saying: In thy seed shall all the kindreds
of the earth be blessed.[44]

Notice how Nephi speaks of the scriptural prophecy that refers to the remnant of the seed of Joseph being "nourished by the Gentiles and being carried in their arms and upon their shoulders." That scripture speaks only metaphorically. The nourishing and carrying can be both literal, but will actually be more symbolic of the assistance and blessings that are prophesied to come to the remnant of the seed of Joseph by those of the Gentiles who receive the Gospel and Priesthood of Jesus Christ. They are numerous and everlasting.

Chapter 7

THE SCATTERING, THEN, THE GATHERING OF ISRAEL BEGINS

We are acquainted with some of the very early history of this area, which was called the Land of Canaan in various parts of the Old Testament. After the children of Israel, as commanded by Jehovah, fought the various other peoples of Canaan, conquered and began living in this area—originally under Joshua—they then had several other leaders.

Under King David, the twelve tribes were unified in the Kingdom of Israel, at around 1,000 B.C. In this united Kingdom of Israel, they had the land divided up into basically twelve parts, or divisions. This remained the case through Solomon's reign as king.

We have already reviewed the rebellion of the northern kingdom against Solomon's son, Rehoboam, in about 922 B.C. That division into northern and southern kingdoms basically continued until 722 B.C., when the Assyrians defeated and carried off captive most of the ten tribes of the northern kingdom.

The Babylonians took over the Assyrian Empire, then conquered the Kingdom of Judah in about 586 B.C.

Some fifty years later, Cyrus, the Persian king took over Babylonia. He allowed certain Jews to return to, settle in, and rebuild Jerusalem.

In about 331 B.C., Alexander the Great conquered the Persian Empire. Eight years later, Alexander died, and the areas he had controlled were divided up among his generals. There was a series of rulers from whom the Jews eventually gained independence. That Jewish state, called Judah, maintained its independence from about 145 to 63 B.C., when the Roman army conquered Judah.

Rome continued to rule the area, despite unsuccessful revolts against their control in 66 A.D. and 132 A. D. Ultimately, the Romans drove the Jews out of Jerusalem by 135 A. D. The Romans then named the area Palestine, after Philistia—the home of the Philistines—who had lived on the south coast of Canaan. Rome retained Palestine for nearly another 500 years.

During the 600s A.D., Arabs conquered Palestine, and retained control until the 1000s, when the Seljuks, part of the Turkish people, got control of Jerusalem in 1071. Their rule lasted fewer than thirty years.

Christian crusaders from Europe fought for Jerusalem for three years, finally capturing Jerusalem in 1099. Christians controlled the city until 1187, when the Muslim leader, Saladin, conquered the city.

Near the mid-1200s, Egyptian rulers, the Marmelukes, took over Palestine as part of their empire, and held on to it until 1517. Then the Ottoman Turks took over. For approximately three hundred years, the Ottoman Turks held control, with Arab Muslims making up most of the population of Palestine. There were only small minorities of Christians and Jews.

In the 1800s, Jews from Europe began to settle in Jerusalem and other parts of Palestine. They wanted to live and die in the Holy Land. By the late 1800s, the oppression of Jews in Europe increased, which resulted in a mass emigration of Jews from various parts of Europe.

The Jews in Palestine wanted to form an independent Jewish nation, which plan the Ottoman government rejected. But the Jews were able to establish some farm colonies in Palestine. As their population increased, so did the population of Arabs in Palestine.

In World War I, Turkey was allied with Germany and Austria-Hungary. Palestine was still ruled by a Turkish military government.

In order to gain Jewish support for Britain's war effort, Britain issued the Balfour Declaration. This stated Britain's support for the creation of an independent Jewish "national home" in Palestine, while still not wanting to violate the rights of non-Jews in the area.

Following the allied nations' victory in World War I, the newly-created League of Nations divided most of the Ottoman Empire into "mandated territories." In 1920, Palestine became a mandated territory of Britain.

Britain was to help the Jews build a national home and to create "self-governing institutions." Initially, this area included areas both west and east of the River Jordan. In 1923, Transjordan (now Jordan) which is east of the river, was separated from the mandate. There was great disagreement over the terms and areas of the mandate.

The Nazis began severe persecutions of the Jews in Germany during the 1930s. Many Jews emigrated from Germany to Palestine.

During World War II, some six million European Jews were killed by the Nazis. Many surviving European Jews were refugees in their countries. Britain, however, maintained limits on the number of Jewish immigrants allowed to come into Palestine. Large Jewish resistance movements pressured Britain to drop the restrictions.

In 1947, Britain requested that the United Nations take over the Palestine problem. A UN special commission recommended the division of Palestine into Jewish and Arab states, with Jerusalem under international control. The UN General Assembly approved this on November 29, 1947. The Jews accepted the plan. The Arabs rejected it.

On May 14, 1948, the Jews proclaimed the independent State of Israel. Britain immediately withdrew from the area. The following day, Arab nations attacked Israel to eliminate the Jewish state. At the end of the fighting, Israel held territory beyond the boundaries of the UN plan. Some 700,000 Arabs fled the Jewish state and became refugees in neighboring Arab countries. Some three years later, the population of Israel included approximately 700,000 Jewish refugees.

Wars occurred between Israel and the surrounding Arab nations in 1949, 1956 and 1967. The war in 1967 was especially remarkable. Pitted against multiple larger Arab countries, the small State of Israel totally wiped out the Arab armies. Israel took over the West Bank, the Gaza Strip and even the Golan Heights of Syria.

In 2018, the population of the State of Israel was nearly nine million.

The above review of the history of the area of Canaan—which became Palestine—which later became Israel clearly shows one major fact. For more than 2,700 years, Israel, which had rejected the Lord, was conquered and controlled by numerous foreign countries and empires.

Then, in 1836, the Prophet Moses:

> . . . committed unto [Joseph Smith] the keys for the gathering of Israel from the four parts of the earth, and the leading of the ten tribes from the land of the north.[45]

As stated herein above, later [i]n the 1800s, Jews from Europe began to settle in Jerusalem and other parts of Palestine. In fewer than a hundred years, Israel had its own state. Just as happened when the children of Israel entered Canaan, following their deliverance from Egypt and its chariot army and its time in the wilderness, the Lord fought Israel's battles.

Think of the Six-day War in 1967 with Israel being threatened by the larger armies of multiple Arab countries, and its amazing—miraculous victory—as we now read for the first of two times, the prophecy of Prophet and President Wilford Woodruff concerning what the Lord will do for Israel. This prophecy literally pertains to the Lord assisting Israel at the end of the War of Armageddon, but His help then seems epilogue—the end of a story—to the prologue—beginning of the story—of earlier latter-day battles that Israel would be required to fight:

> . . . but when this affliction comes, the living God, that led Moses through the wilderness, will deliver you, and your Shiloh will come and stand in your midst and will fight your battles; and you will know him, and the afflictions of the Jews will be at an end, while the destruction of the Gentiles will be so great that it will take the whole house of Israel who are gathered about Jerusalem, seven months to bury the dead of their enemies, and the weapons of war will last them seven years for fuel, so that they need not go to any forest for wood. These are tremendous sayings—who can bear them? Nevertheless they are true, and will be fulfilled, according to the sayings of Ezekiel, Zechariah, and other prophets. Though the heavens and the earth pass away, not one jot or tittle will fall unfilled.[46]

Note: Shiloh is a messianic title for the Messiah, Jesus Christ.

The point I wish to make is that, between the time of the separation of the two kingdoms, northern and southern, in 922 B.C., until 1836, or more than 2,750 years, Israel had struggled, generally losing its battles, often being destroyed, and even being taken away captive. Although struggles did continue, the Jews began to win their battles, be gathered into their ancestral homeland, and soundly defeat their enemies—even though Israel was dramatically outnumbered.

Zechariah describes what the returning—gathered—people of Judah, the Jews, will be like as to those who oppose them.

> 6 ¶ In that day will I make the governors of Judah like an hearth of fire among the wood, and like a torch of fire in a sheaf; and they shall devour all the people round about, on the right hand and on the left: and Jerusalem shall be inhabited again in her own place, *even* in Jerusalem.
> 7 The LORD also shall save the tents of Judah first, that the glory of the house of David and the glory of the inhabitants of Jerusalem do not magnify *themselves* against Judah.
> 8 In that day shall the LORD defend the inhabitants of Jerusalem; and he that is feeble among them at that day shall be as David; and the house of David *shall be* as God, as the angel of the LORD before them.
> 9 ¶ And it shall come to pass in that day, *that* I will seek to destroy all the nations that come against Jerusalem.[47]

So the Jews—Judah—shall devour, or wipe out, all of the people around them who seek their destruction. Jerusalem shall be inhabited by her own people, the Jews. Since June 1967, this has been the case.

The answer to the question, "Why?" is that the prophecies and promises the Lord had given started to be fulfilled. The time in the latter days—becoming the last days—for these promises to come to pass had—has—arrived!

I will venture to say that the Spirit of the Lord has been moving upon the Jewish people since Moses committed the keys to the gathering of Israel in 1836. A sense of that Spirit is obviously evident in the returning of millions of Jews to their homeland in Israel and in the preservation of the State of Israel in its wars against its Arab neighbors. I believe it is also evident in the following short excerpt from the memoir of Abba Eban, Israel's foreign minister in 1967.

As the certainty of war from the surrounding Arab countries, Israel's cabinet voted on June 4, 1967 to give the defense ministry approval to decide when and how to respond to Egypt's aggression. The foreign minister wrote:

> Once we voted, we knew that we had expressed our people's will, for amid the alarms and fears of mid-May, our nation gave birth to new impulses within itself.[48]

He continued, saying in effect that all divisions and fragmentation "seemed to have been transmuted into a new metal which few of us had felt before."[49]

Whenever people are touched by the Holy Spirit, they tend, at least for a time, to become more unified and desirous of peace and common desires. Such seemed to have been the case among the Israeli people.

There has been, and is, another part to the gathering of Israel.

In modern-day Israel, the population is mainly Jewish. So, technically, the gathering has been of the tribe of Judah. But remember, the keys committed by Moses were for the gathering of "Israel," not just Judah. Israel actually includes all twelve (12) tribes. The State of Israel involves primarily Judah, or the Jews.

The gathering of Israel, as just delineated, includes gathering from the four parts of the earth all of the remnants of the tribes of Israel. That process began in 1820, when the Father and the Son appeared to the young man, Joseph Smith. Multiple angelic visitations followed, including to deliver gold plates which would be translated by the gift and power of God into the *Book of Mormon, Another Testament of Jesus Christ*, numerous other revelations, the translation of the *Book of Moses*, the restoration of the priesthood, and the re-establishment of The Church of Jesus Christ to the earth.

Those individuals who have been baptized into The Church of Jesus Christ of Latter-day Saints have come to know of their ancestral heritage, most of whom have some of the blood of Israel in their veins—and are therefore, literally of the House of Israel. The Lord has said that others are adopted into the House of Israel through their baptism into this Church of Jesus Christ of Latter-day Saints.

Therefore, the gathering of Israel has been occurring in at least two (2) remarkable ways. That gathering continues today.

Another form of the gathering of Israel—namely of the tribe of Judah—will occur after Israel and the Jews of the Israeli army are delivered by the Messiah at the conclusion of the War of Armageddon.

This second form of gathering is not a physical gathering to the land of their fathers. The escaping, delivered Jews will look upon the prints in the hands and feet of the Savior, ask where they came from, and following Christ's response, will realize that He is their Savior and Messiah. Their Savior, both literally—physically—and spiritually. There will then follow a mass conversion to the Lord Jesus Christ among the Jews.

Chapter 8

WHAT OTHER PART OF THE HOUSE OF ISRAEL PLAYS A ROLE IN THE GATHERING OF ISRAEL?

You remember that I wrote earlier in this book of there being four separate parts of the House of Israel that would come together in the last days, before the Second Coming of the Lord. They include the ten tribes—both the smaller part thereof who were scattered among the nations of the earth and those of the larger group who were taken into the north countries; the Kingdom of Judah who were taken captive and scattered among all of the nations of the earth; modern-day Saints—those gathered through missionary efforts into The Church of Jesus Christ of Latter-day Saints.

The fourth part includes the seed of Joseph, whose ancestors were led out of Jerusalem in the family of Lehi, whose family was then joined by the family of Ishmael. Eventually, they came across the ocean, settled and lived in the western hemisphere. The righteous from that seed of Joseph will be given this land as their inheritance.

The following quotations refer to the descendants of that part of the House of Israel.

11 For I command all men, both in the east and in the west, and in the north, and in the south, and in the islands of the sea, that they shall write the words which I speak unto them; for out of the books which shall be written I will judge the world, every man according to their works, according to that which is written.

12 For behold, I shall speak unto the Jews and they shall write it; and I shall also speak unto the Nephites and they shall write it; and I shall also speak unto the other tribes of the house of Israel, which I have led away, and they shall write it; and I shall also speak unto all nations of the earth and they shall write it.

13 And it shall come to pass that the Jews shall have the words of the Nephites, and the Nephites shall have the words of the Jews; and the Nephites and the Jews shall have the words of the lost tribes of Israel; and the lost tribes of Israel shall have the words of the Nephites and the Jews.

14 And it shall come to pass that my people, which are of the house of Israel, shall be gathered home unto the lands of their possessions; and my word also shall be gathered in one. And I will show unto them that fight against my word and against my people, who are of the house of Israel, that I am God, and that I covenanted with Abraham that I would remember his seed forever.[50]

An important part of the above verses is the fact that the books containing the teachings given to each of the remnants of the House of Israel shall be brought together by the hand of the Lord. Therefore, the books of scripture written by the Jews, The Holy Bible; by the Nephites, The Book of Mormon; by the seed of Ephraim, The Doctrine and Covenants, and the Pearl of Great Price; as well as the scriptures spoken "unto the other tribes of the house of Israel, which I have led away. . ."

The scriptures of The Church of Jesus Christ of Latter-day Saints—The Book of Mormon—Another Witness of Jesus Christ, The Doctrine and Covenants and The Pearl of Great Price—come from the seed of Ephraim.

We will hereafter—not hereinafter—learn the names and contents of the scriptures revealed to still "other tribes of the house of Israel—the lost ten tribes!

The following verses come from *The Book of Mormon—Another Testament of Jesus Jesus Christ*. Here, the Savior is speaking to the righteous of the Nephites, following His resurrection in Jerusalem. But here, He is visiting them in the land Bountiful, in the New World. He tells them of the other sheep He has who are neither from the land of Jerusalem, nor the land of the Nephites. In other words, He is making reference to the lost ten tribes.

> 12 Ye are my disciples; and ye are a light unto this people, who are a remnant of the house of Joseph.
> 14 And not at any time hath the Father given me commandment that I should tell it unto your brethren at Jerusalem.
> 15 Neither at any time hath the Father given me commandment that I should tell unto them concerning the other tribes of the house of Israel, whom the Father hath led away out of the land.
> 16 This much did the Father command me, that I should tell unto them:
> 17 That other sheep I have which are not of this fold; them also I must bring, and they shall hear my voice; and there shall be one fold, and one shepherd.
> 18 And now, because of stiffneckedness and unbelief they understood not my word; therefore I was commanded to say no more of the Father concerning this thing unto them.
> 19 But, verily, I say unto you that the Father hath commanded me, and I tell it unto you, that ye

> were separated from among them because of their iniquity; therefore it is because of their iniquity that they know not of you.
>
> 20 And verily, I say unto you again that the other tribes hath the Father separated from them; and it is because of their iniquity that they know not of them.
>
> 21 And verily I say unto you, that ye are they of whom I said: Other sheep I have which are not of this fold; them also I must bring, and they shall hear my voice; and there shall be one fold, and one shepherd.
>
> 22 And they understood me not, for they supposed it had been the Gentiles; for they understood not that the Gentiles should be converted through their preaching.
>
> 23 And they understood me not that I said they shall hear my voice; and they understood me not that the Gentiles should not at any time hear my voice—that I should not manifest myself unto them save it were by the Holy Ghost.[51]

After Christ explained that He had not told those in Jerusalem of the Nephites, and that there were in fact others as well—the ten tribes—He told them that He was next going to His Father and also to the lost ten tribes.

> 4 But now I go unto the Father, and also to show myself unto the lost tribes of Israel, for they are not lost unto the Father, for he knoweth whither he hath taken them.[52]

The following verses address the seed of Joseph in the New World, who would be the seed of the Nephites, and especially of the Lamanites—all descendants of Lehi, who was led out from Jerusalem 600 years B.C.

First of all, Israel's (Jacob's) last blessings to his children included this to and about Joseph. He said:

> Joseph is a fruitful bough, even a fruitful bough by a well; whose branches run over the wall; . . .[53]

The bough that is Joseph ran over the wall of the Atlantic Ocean, to the new world. Indeed it was fruitful, like a bough by a well, for there were millions of descendants of Joseph who were born to the Nephites and Lamanites from Manasseh, one of Joseph's sons, the history of whom is found in the Book of Mormon.

The Savior tells the Nephites to whom He had come, that if their seed and the seed of their brethren—the Lamanites—are righteous, they would in the last days have the privilege of assisting many others of the House of Israel in building the New Jerusalem.

> 22 But if they will repent and hearken unto my words, and harden not their hearts, I will establish my church among them, and they shall come in unto the covenant and be numbered among this the remnant of Jacob, unto whom I have given this land for their inheritance;
> 23 And they shall assist my people, the remnant of Jacob, and also as many of the house of Israel as shall come, that they may build a city, which shall be called the New Jerusalem.
> 24 And then shall they assist my people that they may be gathered in, who are scattered upon all the face of the land, in unto the New Jerusalem.
> 25 And then shall the power of heaven come down among them; and I also will be in the midst.
> 26 And then shall the work of the Father commence at that day, even when this gospel shall be preached among the remnant of this people. Verily I say unto you, at that day shall the work of the Father commence among all the dispersed of my

people, yea, even the tribes which have been lost, which the Father hath led away out of Jerusalem.[54]

The Lord speaks of this land, the North American continent, as being "a choice land above all other lands," to which will come down from heaven the holy sanctuary of the Lord—His temple—and the City of New Jerusalem.

1 AND now I, Moroni, proceed to finish my record concerning the destruction of the people of whom I have been writing.

2 For behold, they rejected all the words of Ether; for he truly told them of all things, from the beginning of man; and that after the waters had receded from off the **face of this land it became a choice land above all other lands, a chosen land of the Lord; wherefore the Lord would have that all men should serve him who dwell upon the face thereof;**

3 And that it was the place of the **New Jerusalem, which should come down out of heaven**, and the holy sanctuary of the Lord.

4 Behold, Ether saw the days of Christ, and he spake concerning a New Jerusalem upon this land.

5 And he spake also concerning the house of Israel, and the Jerusalem from whence Lehi should come—after it should be destroyed it should be built up again, a holy city unto the Lord; wherefore, it could not be a new Jerusalem for it had been in a time of old; but it should be built up again, and become a holy city of the Lord; and it should be built unto the house of Israel.

6 And that a New Jerusalem should be built up upon this land, unto the remnant of the seed of Joseph, for which things there has been a type.

7 For as Joseph brought his father down into the land of Egypt, even so he died there; wherefore, the

Lord brought a remnant of the seed of Joseph out of the land of Jerusalem, that he might be merciful unto the seed of Joseph that they should perish not, even as he was merciful unto the father of Joseph that he should perish not.

8 Wherefore, the remnant of the house of Joseph shall be built upon this land; and it shall be a land of their inheritance; and they shall build up a holy city unto the Lord, like unto the Jerusalem of old; and they shall no more be confounded, until the end come when the earth shall pass away.

9 And there shall be a new heaven and a new earth; and they shall be like unto the old save the old have passed away, and all things have become new.

10 And then cometh the New Jerusalem; and blessed are they who dwell therein, for it is they whose garments are white through the blood of the Lamb; and they are they who are numbered among the remnant of the seed of Joseph, who were of the house of Israel.

11 And then also cometh the Jerusalem of old; and the inhabitants thereof, blessed are they, for they have been washed in the blood of the Lamb; and they are they who were scattered and gathered in from the four quarters of the earth, and from the north countries, and are partakers of the fulfilling of the covenant which God made with their father, Abraham.[55]

Those who are righteous enough to be part of that building of the city and temple at the New Jerusalem will have figuratively had their garments made white through the atoning blood of the Savior and Redeemer.

Then, would come also the blessing to Old Jerusalem for those who had been "**scattered and gathered in from the four quarters of the earth**"—the Kingdom of Judah—"**and from the north countries**"—the lost ten tribes of Israel.

Chapter 9

GOD CONTINUES TO FIGHT ISRAEL'S BATTLES

The Prophet Micah writes metaphorically of the trials Israel shall have in the last days with her enemies:

> Be in pain, and labour to bring forth, O daughter of Zion, like a woman in travail: for now shalt thou go forth out of the city, and thou shalt dwell in the field, and thou shalt go *even* to Babylon; there shalt thou be delivered; there the LORD shall redeem thee from the hand of thine enemies.[56]

Using the metaphor of the travail of a woman in labor, prior to the second coming, the world, including the righteous, shall work in pain and tribulation before being delivered by the Lord.

> 11 Now also many nations are gathered against thee, that say, Let her be defiled, and let our eye look upon Zion.
> 12 But they know not the thoughts of the LORD, neither understand they his counsel: for he shall gather them as the sheaves into the floor.
> 13 Arise and thresh, O daughter of Zion: for I will make thine horn iron, and I will make thy hoofs

brass: and thou shalt beat in pieces many people: and I will consecrate their gain unto the LORD, and their substance unto the Lord of the whole earth.[57]

The above verses refer to Jerusalem and modern-day Israel, against which many shall gather and fight, even for three and a half years! As stated in verse 12, those nations who will fight against Jerusalem and Israel will be those who do not understand the Lord, for they do not follow or worship the true Lord God.

Verses 12 and 13 speak metaphorically of what the daughter of Zion, the chosen people of the Lord, the righteous followers of Lord Jesus Christ, shall be able to do at the conclusion of that great battle. The Lord will gather the unrighteous as sheaves of stocks and tares on the floor, and she (they)—the daughter of Zion and (the righteous followers of Christ)—shall thresh the unrighteous. Threshing was done by beating the grain from the chaff on the threshing floor with a flail, a wooden staff with a short heavy stick swinging from it. In other words, she (they) shall beat on the unrighteous, which shall then be separated from the good grain and discarded as useless chaff.

It can be difficult to believe that most or all nations could be against Israel. But after the six-day war in 1967, when all of the Arab nations prepared to attack Israel, and Israel literally "cleaned their plows," totally dominating them in every way, a motion was brought before the United Nations General Assembly. Twenty nations abstained, and the rest voted 99 to 0 to condemn Israel for annexing Jerusalem to its country! Previously, Israel held half of Jerusalem and only over to the Jordan River. Having defeated the Arab invaders, including Jordan, Israel retained the other half of Jerusalem and the rest of the West Bank.

This is only the first time in modern history that the promise from the Lord to Israel has been repeated as was the case after the children of Israel entered Canaan under the leadership of Joshua, following Israel's 40 years of wandering in the wilderness after escaping Egypt, and being delivered from Pharoah's chariot-drawn army at the Red Sea. That promise is:

> The Lord shall fight for you, and ye shall hold your peace.[58]

At the time of the Battle—War—of Armageddon, the Lord shall preserve Israel from the nations of the earth. Zechariah writes:

> Then shall the Lord go forth, and fight against those nations, as when he fought in the day of battle.
> And the Lord shall be king over all the earth; in that day shall there be one Lord, and his name one.[59]

The Doctrine and Covenants also addresses this battle:

> ... for the presence of the Lord shall be as the melting fire that burneth, and as the fire which causeth the waters to boil.
> O Lord, thou shalt come down to make thy name known to thine adversaries, and all nations shall tremble at thy presence.[60]

Once again, President Wilford Woodruff speaks of the Lord fighting the battles of Judah:

> ... but when this affliction comes, the living God, that led Moses through the wilderness, will deliver you, and your Shiloh will come and stand in your midst and will fight your battles; and you will know him, and the afflictions of the Jews will be at an end, while the destruction of the Gentiles will be so great that it will take the whole house of Israel who are gathered about Jerusalem, seven months to bury the dead of their enemies, and the weapons of war will last them seven years for fuel, so that they need not go to any forest for wood. These are tremendous sayings— who can bear them? Nevertheless they are true, and will be fulfilled, according to the sayings of Ezekiel, Zechariah, and other prophets. Though the heavens

and the earth pass away, not one jot or tittle will fall unfulilled.[61]

Christ's second major appearance in His Second Coming will be as foretold in at least two passages of scriptures. We will first read from the Book of Zechariah, Chapter 14. The first three verses speak of the terrible battle in which the Lord, Himself, shall fight against the wicked nations who will be attacking Jerusalem and the Israeli army.

> 1 BEHOLD, the day of the LORD cometh, and thy spoil shall be divided in the midst of thee.
> 2 For I will gather all nations against Jerusalem to battle; and the city shall be taken, and the houses rifled, and the women ravished; and half of the city shall go forth into captivity, and the residue of the people shall not be cut off from the city.
> 3 Then shall the LORD go forth, and fight against those nations, as when he fought in the day of battle.[62]

Verses 4 through 21 speak of the Lord standing upon the mount of Olives, which is the mount which, at the base thereof, on the side facing Jerusalem, is the Garden of Gethsemane. It is right near to the wall of Jerusalem that has the double-arch "Golden Gate". The two—the wall of Jerusalem and the Garden of Gethsemane—are separated only by the very narrow Kidron Valley.

In this work, we will only review verses 4 through 9 of Zechariah Chapter 14.

> 4 ¶ And his feet shall stand in that day upon the mount of Olives, which *is* before Jerusalem on the east, and the mount of Olives shall cleave in the midst thereof toward the east and toward the west, *and there shall be* a very great valley; and half of the mountain shall remove toward the north, and half

of it toward the south.

5 And ye shall flee *to* the valley of the mountains; for the valley of the mountains shall reach unto Azal: yea, ye shall flee, like as ye fled from before the earthquake in the days of Uzziah king of Judah: and the LORD my God shall come, *and* all the saints with thee.

6 And it shall come to pass in that day, *that* the light shall not be clear, *nor* dark:

7 But it shall be one day which shall be known to the LORD, not day, nor night: but it shall come to pass, *that* at evening time it shall be light.

8 And it shall be in that day, *that* living waters shall go out from Jerusalem; half of them toward the former sea, and half of them toward the hinder sea: in summer and in winter shall it be.

9 And the LORD shall be king over all the earth: in that day shall there be one LORD, and his name one.[63]

Verses 10 through 21 are well worth reading, for they tell of how Jerusalem shall be after that day, and what the Lord will expect of those from around Jerusalem (Israel). We will review these verses here, for there is a nice picture painted for those who are righteous, and not a nice one for those who have fought against Jerusalem and the Lord.

10 All the land shall be turned as a plain from Geba to Rimmon south of Jerusalem: and it shall be lifted up, and inhabited in her place, from Benjamin's gate unto the place of the first gate, unto the corner gate, and *from* the tower of Hananeel unto the king's winepresses.

11 And *men* shall dwell in it, and there shall be no more utter destruction; but Jerusalem shall be safely inhabited.

12 ¶ And this shall be the plague wherewith the LORD will smite all the people that have fought

against Jerusalem; Their flesh shall consume away while they stand upon their feet, and their eyes shall consume away in their holes, and their tongue shall consume away in their mouth.

13 And it shall come to pass in that day, *that* a great tumult from the LORD shall be among them; and they shall lay hold every one on the hand of his neighbour, and his hand shall rise up against the hand of his neighbour.

14 And Judah also shall fight at Jerusalem; and the wealth of all the heathen round about shall be gathered together, gold, and silver, and apparel, in great abundance.

15 And so shall be the plague of the horse, of the mule, of the camel, and of the ass, and of all the beasts that shall be in these tents, as this plague.

16 ¶ And it shall come to pass, *that* every one that is left of all the nations which came against Jerusalem shall even go up from year to year to worship the King, the LORD of hosts, and to keep the feast of tabernacles.

17 And it shall be, *that* whoso will not come up of *all* the families of the earth unto Jerusalem to worship the King, the LORD of hosts, even upon them shall be no rain.

18 And if the family of Egypt go not up, and come not, that *have* no *rain;* there shall be the plague, wherewith the LORD will smite the heathen that come not up to keep the feast of tabernacles.

19 This shall be the punishment of Egypt, and the punishment of all nations that come not up to keep the feast of tabernacles.

20 ¶ In that day shall there be upon the bells of the horses, HOLINESS UNTO THE LORD; and the pots in the LORD's house shall be like the bowls

> before the altar.
> 21 Yea, every pot in Jerusalem and in Judah shall be holiness unto the LORD of hosts: and all they that sacrifice shall come and take of them, and seethe therein: and in that day there shall be no more the Canaanite in the house of the LORD of hosts.[64]

This second appearance of the Lord as part of His Second Coming is also foretold in The Doctrine and Covenants, Section 45:47-59. The nineteen (19) verses from verse 28 through 46, give great information about the gospel being restored, the times of the Gentiles being fulfilled, and the signs of the times being given. So, we will first look at many of the verses 28 through 46, then verses 47 through 53. Lastly, we will review verses 54 through 59. These verses tell of what will take place right at that time.

> 28 And when the times of the Gentiles is come in, a light shall break forth among them that sit in darkness, and it shall be the fulness of my gospel;
> 30 And in that generation shall the times of the Gentiles be fulfilled.
> 31 And there shall be men standing in that generation, that shall not pass until they shall see an overflowing scourge; for a desolating sickness shall cover the land.
> 32 But my disciples shall stand in holy places, and shall not be moved; but among the wicked, men shall lift up their voices and curse God and die.
> 33 And there shall be earthquakes also in divers places, and many desolations; yet men will harden their hearts against me, and they will take up the sword, one against another, and they will kill one another.
> 35 And I said unto them: **Be not troubled, for, when all these things shall come to pass, ye may know that the promises which have been made unto**

you shall be fulfilled.

36 And when the light shall begin to break forth, it shall be with them like unto a parable which I will show you—

37 Ye look and behold the fig-trees, and ye see them with your eyes, and ye say when they begin to shoot forth, and their leaves are yet tender, that summer is now nigh at hand;

38 Even so it shall be in that day when they shall see all these things, then shall they know that the hour is nigh.

39 And it shall come to pass that he that feareth me shall be looking forth for the great day of the Lord to come, even for the signs of the coming of the Son of Man.

40 And they shall see signs and wonders, for they shall be shown forth in the heavens above, and in the earth beneath.

41 And they shall behold blood, and fire, and vapors of smoke.

42 And before the day of the Lord shall come, the sun shall be darkened, and the moon be turned into blood, and the stars fall from heaven.

43 And the remnant shall be gathered unto this place;

44 And then they shall look for me, and, behold, I will come; and they shall see me in the clouds of heaven, clothed with power and great glory; with all the holy angels; and he that watches not for me shall be cut off.

45 But before the arm of the Lord shall fall, an angel shall sound his trump, and the saints that have slept shall come forth to meet me in the cloud.

46 Wherefore, if ye have slept in peace blessed are you; for as you now behold me and know that I am, even so shall ye come unto me and your souls shall live, and your redemption shall be perfected; and the

saints shall come forth from the four quarters of the earth.

47 Then shall the arm of the Lord fall upon the nations.

48 And then shall the Lord set his foot upon this mount, and it shall cleave in twain, and the earth shall tremble, and reel to and fro, and the heavens also shall shake.

49 And the Lord shall utter his voice, and all the ends of the earth shall hear it; and the nations of the earth shall mourn, and they that have laughed shall see their folly.

50 And calamity shall cover the mocker, and the scorner shall be consumed; and they that have watched for iniquity shall be hewn down and cast into the fire.

51 And then shall the Jews look upon me and say: What are these wounds in thine hands and in thy feet?

52 Then shall they know that I am the Lord; for I will say unto them: These wounds are the wounds with which I was wounded in the house of my friends. I am he who was lifted up. I am Jesus that was crucified. I am the Son of God.

53 And then shall they weep because of their iniquities; then shall they lament because they persecuted their king.

55 And Satan shall be bound, that he shall have no place in the hearts of the children of men.

56 And at that day, when I shall come in my glory, shall the parable be fulfilled which I spake concerning the ten virgins.

57 For they that are wise and have received the truth, and have taken the Holy Spirit for their guide, and have not been deceived—verily I say unto you, they shall not be hewn down and cast into the fire, but shall abide the day.

>   58 And the earth shall be given unto them for an inheritance; and they shall multiply and wax strong, and their children shall grow up without sin unto salvation.
>   59 For the Lord shall be in their midst, and his glory shall be upon them, and he will be their king and their lawgiver.[65] (Emphasis added.)

We have read earlier in this book of the Lord fighting Israel's battles, as He did for the children of Israel at the time Joshua led them across the River Jordan into the land of Canaan. We have also spoken of how the Lord has obviously assisted the modern-day State of Israel as it has had to battle for its very existence on multiple occasions. He will continue to fight the battles for Israel, for those who oppose Israel and the Lord will be the wicked of the world, whose unrighteous desires and goals shall not stand.

GLEN W. PARK

Chapter 10

TWO PROPHETS FIGHT FOR ISRAEL

In these last days, the Lord continues to fight battles for Israel. In this chapter, we will read of a new and especially interesting circumstance in His assisting His people, Israel.

In The Doctrine and Covenants, the Lord answers questions posed by the Prophet Joseph Smith. In particular, there follow the question and answer concerning a circumstance that will occur just before the Lord's Second Coming. This is the last question and answer in Section 77, Verse 15 of The Doctrine and Covenants.

> Q. What is to be understood by the two witnesses, in the eleventh chapter of Revelation?
>
> A. They are two prophets that are to be raised up to the Jewish nation in the last days, at the time of the restoration, and to prophesy to the Jews after they are gathered and have built the city of Jerusalem in the land of their fathers.[66]

It is worthwhile to read what these two prophets can and will do, and what will eventually happen to them.

Another similar, significant prophecy in Revelation is found in Chapter 11. This prophecy tells us of those same two (2) witnesses in Israel during the forty-two month, three and a half year battle or war of Armageddon. Let us read the eleven (11) verses that help us understand the evil nature of the nations who will be fighting against Jerusalem and Israel, the great power of the two witnesses, what initially happens to those two witnesses, what ultimately happens to those witnesses, and what ultimately happens to those who fight against Israel.

> 3 And I will give *power* unto my two witnesses, and they shall prophesy a thousand two hundred *and* threescore days, clothed in sackcloth.
> 4 These are the two olive trees, and the two candlesticks standing before the God of the earth.
> 5 And if any man will hurt them, fire proceedeth out of their mouth, and devoureth their enemies: and if any man will hurt them, he must in this manner be killed.
> 6 These have power to shut heaven, that it rain not in the days of their prophecy: and have power over waters to turn them to blood, and to smite the earth with all plagues, as often as they will.
> 7 And when they shall have finished their testimony, the beast that ascendeth out of the bottomless pit shall make war against them, and shall overcome them, and kill them.
> 8 And their dead bodies *shall lie* in the street of the great city, which spiritually is called Sodom and Egypt, where also our Lord was crucified.
> 9 And they of the people and kindreds and tongues and nations shall see their dead bodies three days and an half, and shall not suffer their dead bodies to be put in graves.
> 10 And they that dwell upon the earth shall rejoice over them, and make merry, and shall send gifts one to another; because these two prophets

> tormented them that dwelt on the earth.
>
> 11 And after three days and a half the Spirit of life from God entered into them, and they stood upon their feet; and great fear fell upon them which saw them.
>
> 12 And they heard a great voice from heaven saying unto them, Come up hither. And they ascended up to heaven in a cloud; and their enemies beheld them.
>
> 13 And the same hour was there a great earthquake, and the tenth part of the city fell, and in the earthquake were slain of men seven thousand: and the remnant were affrighted, and gave glory to the God of heaven.[67]

This is an amazing prophecy. Let me set the stage for this a little more. Remember, most or all nations of the world will amass to battle Jerusalem and Israel for a period of forty-two months, or three and a half years. These are wicked nations. This is an unholy, wicked war. The Lord does not look kindly upon the wicked—even evil—men and nations responsible for this war against His chosen people.

The Lord assists those in Jerusalem and Israel through these two prophets—also called, or referred to, as "witnesses", "olive trees" and "candlesticks." In fact, great power is given to the two. I will simply list the gifts of power they will have:

1 – Fire from their mouths devours their enemies.

2 – If anyone hurts them, that (those) person(s) shall die in the same manner as did the hurt he(they) caused.

3 – They can shut the heaven, stopping the rain.

4 - They can turn waters to blood.

5 - They can cause any plague, when they desire.

Numbers 6, 7 and 8 will be written after the following three short paragraphs.

We read that, after they had finished their testimony, the devil will make war against them, overcome them and kill them.

After their death, they are not buried almost immediately, as is the practice among both the Jewish and Muslims. Instead, their enemies try to heap disgrace upon them, by leaving their dead bodies to lie in the street for three and a half days.

Their wicked enemies celebrate their death and even send gifts to each other for their seeming victory over the two witnesses.

6 - The Spirit of life from God enters them, they stand up, and everyone around them—all of whom are their enemies—are rightfully scared to death.

7 – They are called—raised—up to heaven, which their enemies see.

8 – At the same time, a great earthquake occurs and seven thousand of their enemies are killed. Those who remain are even more frightened, and acknowledge that it is the true God that has done this.

The Lord could stop this war, but He will allow it as He has throughout the history of the world. Why? Although it could be accurately said that there are many, many reasons, I will present the three (3) primary reasons for the righteous to be allowed to suffer through these tribulations, as well as, other trials. I will also present the two (2) primary reasons why the Lord allows the wicked to pursue such things, although they are wicked.

As to the righteous who must wade through and endure these horrible tribulations:

1 – Many lessons, including substantial spiritual knowledge and experiences will come to the righteous through their reaction to, and endurance of, their trials.

2 – As the righteous faithfully endure immense trials and tribulations, they prove themselves worthy of, and **become** more like, Christ, thereby becoming worthy of eternal life and exaltation.

3 – Those seemingly righteous, who are unable to continue to faithfully endure, and either cease striving to be worthy, and/or those who wind up murmuring and rebelling against the Lord, prove themselves not righteous or worthy enough to receive the wonderful blessings promised by the Lord for the truly righteous.

As to the unrighteous who actually are among the cause of many of these horrible tribulations:

1 – Since some of the unrighteous—also called "wicked"— on the way to those who are evil, may, as did the citizens of Nineveh, repent after a plague, followed by a civil war. So, the preaching done to them by the Lord, Himself, via plague and the sword, ended up being pretty persuasive. I believe, that some of the unrighteous will repent during these times of tribulation.

2 – The wicked and the evil humans, if they do not repent, will, by the horrible and evil things they do, prove without question that they deserve to be cast out—to be those who will go to the telestial kingdom, and even some of them be so evil as to drink the dregs of the cup of the wrath of God—the bottom, worst part of that lowest kingdom that is not part of the place where go the Sons of Perdition.

Chapter 11

WHAT ABOUT THE CITY OF ENOCH? WHEN AND TO WHERE WILL IT RETURN?

You may wonder, what have the City of Enoch and its people to do with the restoration of the lost ten tribes? I can name two reasons that make them relevant in this book:

1 – We know that the lost ten tribes shall be miraculously restored to the earth and help with the "cleaning up of the earth and the building of one, and perhaps both, of the temples addressed in this book. The City of Enoch shall return to the earth and assist in the building of the City of New Jerusalem and the temple there. So the lost ten tribes and the people of the City of Enoch may be involved together in those righteous enterprises.

2 – Some have wondered if the return of those two sets of peoples would occur together.

My view of these two matters is primarily formed from my review of the scriptures and prophetic statements that follow in this chapter. In a sentence, I believe reason #1 above, and as to #2, I believe their return shall be separate one from the other. Let us read the following relevant citations.

The Apostle Orson F. Whitney spoke of the return of the City of Enoch:

> The gathered Saints are up here in the Rocky Mountains, out of harm's way comparatively speaking, founding Stakes of Zion, as a preliminary to the establishment of Zion proper; and we shall remain here until our preparation is complete. When the right time comes, and all things are ready, the pure in heart, chosen from the midst of the people, will go down in the might of the Lord and redeem Zion. Then shall the New Jerusalem be built, and the way prepared for the return of the City of Enoch and for the glorious coming of the Lord.[68]

The Apostle Orson Pratt also spoke of this:

> You know in the days of Enoch the Lord placed the people upon the high places and mountains, and they flourished, and He blessed them, and called them Zion because there was no poor among them, and the Lord was in their midst. Now the Latter-day Zion is to be built up according to the same pattern, so far as circumstances will permit, for we expect that the Zion which was built up by Enoch, that had no poor in it, will come down again at the commencement of the Millennium to meet the Zion here, according to the song in the Book of Covenants. "The Lord has brought up Zion from beneath, the Lord has brought down Zion from above," and they shall gaze upon each other's countenances, and see eye to eye.[69]

The Book of Moses is an extract from the translation of the Bible as revealed to the Prophet Joseph Smith between June 1830 and February 1831. In the following verses, the Lord tells somewhat of the circumstances at the time of Enoch's teaching the people who came to be known as the City of Enoch. In Genesis, there are only six (6) verses concerning Enoch and his people. In the restored Book of Moses, there are well over one hundred (100) verses.

Those around the City of Enoch were wicked and involved in wars. But because of the Spirit of the Lord attended the people of Enoch, others around them were afraid to confront them.

> 16 And from that time forth there were wars and bloodshed among them; but the Lord came and dwelt with his people, and they dwelt in righteousness.
> 17 The fear of the Lord was upon all nations, so great was the glory of the Lord, which was upon his people. And the Lord blessed the land, and they were blessed upon the mountains, and upon the high places, and did flourish.
> 18 And the Lord called his people ZION, because they were of one heart and one mind, and dwelt in righteousness; and there was no poor among them.
> 19 And Enoch continued his preaching in righteousness unto the people of God. And it came to pass in his days, that he built a city that was called the City of Holiness, even ZION.
> 20 And it came to pass that Enoch talked with the Lord; and he said unto the Lord: Surely Zion shall dwell in safety forever. But the Lord said unto Enoch: Zion have I blessed, but the residue of the people have I cursed.
> 21 And it came to pass that the Lord showed unto Enoch all the inhabitants of the earth; and he beheld, and lo, Zion, in process of time, was taken up into heaven. And the Lord said unto Enoch: Behold mine abode forever.[70]

The Lord speaks through the Prophet Joseph, as recorded in The Doctrine and Covenants, that it was He who took unto Himself the Zion—City—of Enoch. Later references shall reveal more concerning that City and its people.

> I am the same which have taken the Zion of Enoch into mine own bosom; and verily, I say, even as many as have believed in my name, for I am Christ, and in mine own name, by the virtue of the blood which I have spilt, have I pleaded before the Father for them.[71]

The Lord next speaks generally of the City of Enoch, and of the time for which that city has been reserved:

> 11 Wherefore, hearken ye together and let me show unto you even my wisdom—the wisdom of him whom ye say is the God of Enoch, and his brethren,
> 12 Who were separated from the earth, and were received unto myself—a city reserved until a day of righteousness shall come—a day which was sought for by all holy men, and they found it not because of wickedness and abominations;[72]

Next, we read what is referred to as the song of The Doctrine and Covenants, found in Section 84. In these two verses, we read of Zion—here meaning the City of Enoch—having been redeemed because of the peoples' faith and covenant. Then, in verse 100, the Lord refers to the time when Satan is bound—which is during the Millennium. Then, that this city—Zion—has been brought down, back to Earth from above. And, Zion—the righteous Saints already on Earth, has been brought from beneath—under heaven.

> 99 The Lord hath brought again Zion;
> The Lord hath redeemed his people, Israel,
> According to the election of grace,
> Which was brought to pass by the faith

And covenant of their fathers.
>100 The Lord hath redeemed his people;
And Satan is bound and time is no longer.
The Lord hath gathered all things in one.
The Lord hath brought down Zion from above.
The Lord hath brought up Zion from beneath.[73]

The two verses above imply that these two Zion peoples will come together. Therefore, one would not assume that the one would come with others—namely, with the lost ten tribes.

The next verses, also from the Book of Moses, speak of the City of New Jerusalem, and that the City of Enoch and its people shall meet the righteous Saints there.

> 62 And righteousness will I send down out of heaven; and truth will I send forth out of the earth, to bear testimony of mine Only Begotten; his resurrection from the dead; yea, and also the resurrection of all men; and righteousness and truth will I cause to sweep the earth as with a flood, to gather out mine elect from the four quarters of the earth, unto a place which I shall prepare, an Holy City, that my people may gird up their loins, and be looking forth for the time of my coming; **for there shall be my tabernacle, and it shall be called Zion, a New Jerusalem.**
> 63 **And the Lord said unto Enoch: Then shalt thou and all thy city meet them there**, and we will receive them into our bosom, and they shall see us; and we will fall upon their necks, and they shall fall upon our necks, and we will kiss each other;
> 64 And there shall be mine abode, and it shall be Zion, which shall come forth out of all the creations which I have made; and for the space of a thousand years the earth shall rest.[74]
> (Emphasis added.)

Chapter 12

WHERE ARE THE LOST TEN TRIBES?

Granted, the above chapter title seems like a silly question. If they are the "**lost**" ten tribes, then aren't they lost? If they are "lost," that would logically mean that they have not been found that their location is unknown.

We do know that they are not lost to the Father. Since the Savior went to visit them, then they are also not lost to the Son. But they are lost to the world—for the most part, that is. The Savior, at the end of His visit to the Nephites, following His resurrection, said:

> But now I go unto the Father, and also to show myself unto the lost tribes of Israel, for they are not lost unto the Father, for he knoweth whither he hath taken them.[75]

Although it has not been revealed **exactly** where they are, we will now read **generally** where they were taken. At least we know basically where they are, and we will read hereinafter how, and basically when, they will be restored. There follow multiple accounts of latter-day scriptures, prophets, apostles and other Church authorities and historians who address the question of the location of the lost ten tribes.

Eliza R. Snow wrote more than one hymn that deal with this subject. Part of one will follow later in this chapter. This first one reflects light and knowledge she received from listening to the Prophet Joseph Smith.

> Thou earth wast once a glorious sphere of noble
> magnitude,
> And didst with majesty appear among the worlds
> of God.
> But thy dimensions have been torn asunder
> piece by piece,
> And each dismembered fragment borne abroad
> to distant space.
> When Enoch could no longer stay amid
> corruption here,
> Part of thyself wast borne away to form
> another sphere.
> That portion where his city stood he gained by
> right approved;
> And nearer to the throne of God his planet
> upward moved.
> And when the Lord saw fit to hide the Ten
> Lost Tribes away,
> Thou, earth, wast severed to provide an orb on
> which they stay.
> And thus from time to time thy size hast been
> diminished till
> Thou seemest the law of sacrifice created to
> fulfill.
> A restitution yet must come that will to thee
> restore
> By grand law of world, thy sum of matter
> heretofore."[76]

The former Apostle Mark E. Petersen spoke of the lost ten tribes. He said:

I do not believe we should accept the current views that the lost ten tribes have been found in the northern nations of Europe or that they have been named, indexed, and classified. I do not believe that we can accept the peculiar notion that the mythical Odin of the North was in reality the Savior of the world performing his work among the northern nations of Europe or the ten tribes.[77]

You have already read concerning the type of place—in relation to the earth—where the larger part of the lost ten tribes were taken. In The Doctrine and Covenants, Section 133, we can read of some of the changes to the earth that shall take place at their return:

> 23 He shall command the great deep, and it shall be driven back into the north countries, and the islands shall become one land;
> 24 And the land of Jerusalem and the land of Zion shall be turned back into their own place, and the earth shall be like as it was in the days before it was divided.
> 25 And the Lord, even the Savior, shall stand in the midst of his people, and shall reign over all flesh.
> 26 And they who are in the north countries shall come in remembrance before the Lord; and their prophets shall hear his voice, and shall no longer stay themselves; and they shall smite the rocks, and the ice shall flow down at their presence.
> 27 And an highway shall be cast up in the midst of the great deep.[78]

The Doctrine and Covenants continues to describe more of what will happen when the lost ten tribes return.

> 28 Their enemies shall become a prey unto them,

> 29 And in the barren deserts there shall come forth pools of living water; and the parched ground shall no longer be a thirsty land.
> 30 And they shall bring forth their rich treasures unto the children of Ephraim, my servants.
> 31 And the boundaries of the everlasting hills shall tremble at their presence.
> 32 And there shall they fall down and be crowned with glory, even in Zion, by the hands of the servants of the Lord, even the children of Ephraim.
> 33 And they shall be filled with songs of everlasting joy.
> 34 Behold, this is the blessing of the everlasting God upon the tribes of Israel, and the richer blessing upon the head of Ephraim and his fellows.[79]

We have just read some very significant facts that will accompany their restoration.

Any enemies shall be more than just defeated. Let us dissect this verse 28. The scripture does not say that the ten tribes shall be victorious over their enemies. When one considers "prey", the image is of a lion attacking, killing and eating some smaller, weaker animal. This situation is not of two near-equals battling it out, with one eventually becoming the victor, possibly suffering much injury itself. No, the enemies of the ten tribes shall simply fall before them.

Verse 29 tells us that dry, barren deserts shall have pools of living water come forth. Such could be the result of the earthquake(s) that are to occur at their return.

In verse 30, we read that the ten tribes shall bring their "rich treasures" unto God's servants, Ephraim. There are two parts to what we learn from this verse:

1 – The lost ten tribes shall bring their "rich treasures." This almost certainly refers to their scriptures. These would be their historical and spiritual record of nearly three thousand years!

2 – Ephraim refers to the modern "birthright" tribe, which prophets and apostles explain is the leadership, and bulk of the membership of, The Church of Jesus Christ of Latter-day Saints.

The next four verses we just read explain why the lost tribes shall bring their treasures unto Ephraim.

Verse 31 teaches us where the lost ten tribes shall go (come) with their treasures—to the everlasting hills, which "shall tremble at their presence." The everlasting hills begin at the northernmost part of North America, and extend to the southern tip of South America—thus appearing to be "everlasting", or without beginning or end.

Within this mountain range are the current headquarters of The Church of Jesus Christ of Latter-day Saints. Thus, these everlasting hills shall tremble at the coming of the lost ten tribes, who will come to these mountains to find Ephraim.

In verses 32 through 34, we are told that the lost ten tribes shall there fall down and be crowned with glory, even in Zion. They shall humble themselves and receive their priesthood and temple blessings at the hands of the children of Ephraim—through the keys to priesthood authority held by the prophets and apostles of The Church of Jesus Christ of Latter-day Saints. Those temple blessings—ordinances with covenants—shall provide them with what is essential for those tribes to receive eternal life with the Father and the Son.

Obviously, the lost tribes shall sing with joy over those wonderful and eternal blessings which then can be theirs.

Now, we will read the explanations and revealed words of modern-day prophets, apostles and other priesthood leaders, which will help us better understand where the lost ten tribes were taken, and information of their restoration to the earth.

Here follows a statement from Joseph Smith, made on June 3, 1831 at a conference of the Church:

John the Revelator was then among the Ten Tribes of Israel who had been led away by Shalmaneser, king of Assyria, to prepare them for their return from their long dispersion.[80]

Wilford Woodruff recorded in his journal in 1856:

Here, President Young is quoted as saying that the ten tribes of Israel are on a portion of the earth—a portion separated from the main land.[81]

The Apostle Parley P. Pratt spoke of the return of the lost ten tribes, of the stars falling and of the days of Enoch and perhaps of Peleg. In doing so, he helps us understand the separation of parts of the earth in earlier times. He wrote by way of questions and answers in 1841.

Ques. 7th.- How can the stars fall from heaven to earth, when they (as far as we know) are much larger than the earth?

Ans.- We are nowhere given to understand that all the stars will fall or even many of them: but only "as a fig tree casteth her UNTIMELY figs when she is shaken with a mighty wind." The stars, which will fall to the earth, are fragments, which have been broken off from the earth from time to time, in the mighty convulsions of nature. Some in the days of Enoch, some perhaps in the days of Peleg, some with the ten tribes, and some at the crucifixion of the Messiah. These all must be restored again at the "times of restitution of ALL THINGS." This will restore the ten tribes of Israel; and also bring again Zion, even Enoch's city. It will bring back the tree of life, which is in the midst of the paradise of God; that you and I may partake of it. [See Rev.11, 7.] When these fragments (some of which are vastly larger than the present earth) are brought back and joined to this earth, it will cause a convulsion of all nature, the graves of the Saints will be opened, and they rise from the dead; while the mountains will flow down, the valleys rise, the sea retire to its own place, the islands and continents will be removed, and earth be rolled together as a scroll. . . . [82]

Jacob Gates, a member of the First Council of the Seventy in the 1800s, wrote this in one of his journals:

. . . he heard Joseph Smith say when he was at Bishop Partridge's house in Far West, Missouri, concerning the ten lost tribes, they are hid from us by land and air. Said Bishop Partridge, "I guess they are hid by land and water," in a doubting manner as if Joseph did not know what he was talking about. "Yes," said Joseph, "by land and air; they are hid from us in such a manner and at such an angle that the astronomers cannot get their telescopes to bear on them from this earth."[83]

Elder Jacob Gates also recorded the information he received when he visited Sister Eliza R. Snow. He wrote:

At night paid Sister Eliza R. Snow a short visit and had some conversation with her on the dividing of the earth. She told me that she heard the Prophet Joseph say that when the 10 tribes were taken away, the Lord cut the earth in two, Joseph striking his left hand in the center with the edge of his right to illustrate the idea, and that they (the 10 tribes) were on an orb or planet by themselves, and when they returned with the portion of this earth that was taken away with them, the coming together of these two bodies or orbs would cause a shock and make the "earth reel to and fro like a drunken man." She also stated that he said the earth was . . . ninety times smaller now than when it was first created or organized."[84]

Chapter 13

THE RETURN— RESTORATION—OF THE TEN TRIBES

In prior chapters, we have read scriptures and discussed the division of the tribes of Israel into two separate kingdoms and of the disobedience of the northern kingdom—Israel—comprised of ten of the twelve tribes.

We also have read of the defeat by the Assyrians of the northern kingdom of Israel, as well as, the captivity of Israel that was imposed upon that kingdom by Assyria.

Let us read prophecies of the restoration, or return of the ten tribes of Israel which were lost to the world.

> In those days the house of Judah shall walk with the house of Israel, and they shall come together out of the land of the north to the land that I have given for an inheritance unto your fathers.[85]

Here, the Prophet Jeremiah speaks of the time in the last days when the two kingdoms of the children of Israel—Judah and Israel, shall return to the land originally given to their fathers—in and around modern-day Israel.

Jeremiah continues explaining how remarkable and amazing will be the Lord's bringing back the lost ten tribes from the place where they have tarried all of these centuries since they were taken captive and removed from the land of Israel in 722 B.C. So we read again the verses that give explanation that we have previously read concerning His miraculous restoration of the lost ten tribes.

14 ¶ Therefore, behold, the days come, saith the LORD, that it shall no more be said, The LORD liveth, that brought up the children of Israel out of the land of Egypt;
15 But, The LORD liveth, that brought up the children of Israel from the land of the north, and from all the lands whither he had driven them: and I will bring them again into their land that I gave unto their fathers.
16 ¶ Behold, I will send for many fishers, saith the LORD, and they shall fish them; and after will I send for many hunters, and they shall hunt them from every mountain, and from every hill, and out of the holes of the rocks.
17 For mine eyes *are* upon all their ways: they are not hid from my face, neither is their iniquity hid from mine eyes.
18 And first I will recompense their iniquity and their sin double; because they have defiled my land, they have filled mine inheritance with the carcases of their detestable and abominable things.
19 O LORD, my strength, and my fortress, and my refuge in the day of affliction, the Gentiles shall come unto thee from the ends of the earth, and shall say, Surely our fathers have inherited lies, vanity, and

> *things* wherein *there is* no profit.
> 20 Shall a man make gods unto himself, and they *are* no gods?
> 21 Therefore, behold, I will this once cause them to know, I will cause them to know mine hand and my might; and they shall know that my name *is* The LORD.[86]

In the 31st chapter of Jeremiah, the Lord tells us that it will be a very large number of people of the lost ten tribes that He will bring from the north countries. They will be brought in a company, not one-by-one.

> 7 For thus saith the LORD; Sing with gladness for Jacob, and shout among the chief of the nations: publish ye, praise ye, and say, O LORD, save thy people, the remnant of Israel.
> 8 Behold, I will bring them from the north country, and gather them from the coasts of the earth, *and* with them the blind and the lame, the woman with child and her that travaileth with child together: a great company shall return thither.
> 9 They shall come with weeping, and with supplications will I lead them: I will cause them to walk by the rivers of waters in a straight way, wherein they shall not stumble: for I am a father to Israel, and Ephraim *is* my firstborn.
> 10 ¶ Hear the word of the LORD, O ye nations, and declare *it* in the isles afar off, and say, He that scattered Israel will gather him, and keep him, as a shepherd *doth* his flock.
> 11 For the LORD hath redeemed Jacob, and ransomed him from the hand of *him that was* stronger than he.
> 12 Therefore they shall come and sing in the height of Zion, and shall flow together to the

goodness of the LORD, for wheat, and for wine, and for oil, and for the young of the flock and of the herd: and their soul shall be as a watered garden; and they shall not sorrow any more at all.[87]

The Lord will bring in a significant company the ten tribes from the north countries. Moreover, Ephraim, one of the sons of Joseph, who was sold into Egypt, will be given the birthright of the firstborn among the twelve tribes of Israel.

The height of Zion needs to be distinguished from Zion, the city of the New Jerusalem. They are not at all the same place. Thus, the height of Zion—Mount Zion—is next to Old Jerusalem, in present-day Israel. As stated elsewhere in this book, Zion, the New Jerusalem, is found in the State of Missouri, in the United States of America.

First of all, the height of Zion refers to the top of Mount Zion, located south of Zion Gate, near the southwest corner of East Jerusalem. At the time of the creation of the State of Israel in 1948, East Jerusalem was part of the State of Jordan.

Mount Zion was in Israeli territory, as stated above, just south of the southwest part of East Jerusalem. This mount rises from the Valley of Hinnom (Gehenna), immediately to the south of Mount Zion.

Remember:

> For out of Zion shall go forth the law, and the word of the Lord from Jerusalem.[88]

The "Zion" referred to in the quotation above, is the New Jerusalem.

There are in the above quotation, two separate items—the law and the word of the Lord. There are also two separate locations—the New Jerusalem in Missouri, and the Old Jerusalem in modern-day Israel.

Flavius Josephus, concerning the ten tribes, records what he sees as the fact that:

> ... the ten tribes are beyond the Euphrates till now, and are an immense multitude and not to be estimated in numbers.[89]

The Romano-Jewish historian, Flavius Josephus, described, as you have just read, that the numbers in the ten tribes are "immense."

The Apostle Parley P. Pratt wrote of the return of the lost ten tribes, as follows:

> Here you behold an ensign to be reared for the nations; not only for the dispersed of Judah, but the outcast of Israel. The Jews are called dispersed, because they are scattered among the nations; but the ten tribes are called outcasts, because they are cast out from the knowledge of the nations into a land by themselves. Now, the reader will bear in mind that the ten tribes have not dwelt in the land of Canaan since they were led captive by Shalmanezer, king of Assyria. We have also presented before us, . . . the marvelous power of God, which will be displayed in the destruction of a small branch of the Red Sea, called the tongue of the Egyptian Sea: and also the dividing of the seven streams of some river, and causing men to go over dry shod; and lest any should not understand it literally, the next verse says, "there shall be an highway for the remnant of his people, which shall be left, from Assyria; like as it was to Israel to the day that he came up out of the land of Egypt."[90]

He then referred to the scripture written in this book about Israel no longer speaking of the Lord's bringing the children of Israel out of Egypt, because of remarkable event(s) when the ten tribes are restored. Then he continued:

> ... They will exclaim, The Lord liveth, which recently brought the children of Israel from the north, and from all lands whither he had driven them, and hath planted them in the land of Canaan, which he gave our fathers. With this idea will be associated every display of grandeur and sublimity, of wonder and amazement; while they call to mind the revelations, manifestations, miracles, and mercies displayed in bringing about this great event, in the eyes of all nations.[91]

How righteous would we assume that the lost ten tribes will be just before the Lord's Second Coming? My thoughts on that subject follow.

After His crucifixion and resurrection, Jesus Christ showed Himself to the righteous Nephites in the Land Bountiful, as the Book of Third Nephi records. He taught the people there, healed their sick of all kinds of sickness. He called twelve disciples, taught them the mode and words for baptism and bestowed upon His disciples the priesthood authority to baptize and bestow the Gift of the Holy Ghost. Then He told them that He was going to go to visit the lost ten tribes. Let us again read the account:

> But now I go unto the Father, and also to show myself unto the lost tribes of Israel, for they are not lost unto the Father, for he knoweth whither he hath taken them.[92]

We know that when those ten tribes were conquered and taken captive by the Assyrians, it was because of their unrighteousness. As stated in this book, we know that they were taken to Assyria. In time, a part of them were scattered to other nations, eventually to most or all nations of the earth.

The larger remnant of those ten tribes were then taken into "the north countries," and "lost" to the world. But as the above verse tells us, "they are not lost to the Father, for he knoweth whither he hath taken them." So, after visiting the Nephites, Christ proceeded to go visit the lost ten tribes.

We know from the Book of Mormon that, after the Savior's visit, the people of the Americas lived in peace, prosperity and righteousness for some two hundred years! Why? First of all, the wicked and evil had been killed off by the destruction that occurred there at the time of the death of the Savior in Jerusalem. Secondly, the influence and effect upon the hearts and minds of the righteous survivors of seeing and hearing the Savior, and having their spirits converted to His gospel, were so profound.

Now we can re-focus on the lost ten tribes, who had been taken because of their wickedness. Although we have not been specifically told this, my belief is that the Savior's visit to the lost ten tribes had the same type of effect on those people. Most likely, He taught the people there, healed their sick and afflicted. He called disciples, taught the mode and words for baptism and bestowed upon them the priesthood authority to baptize and bestow the Gift of the Holy Ghost. Thereafter, the influence and effect upon the hearts and minds of the righteous survivors there, of seeing and hearing the Savior, and having their spirits converted to His gospel were likely to have been equally profound as it had been upon the Nephites.

How long that effect upon the lost ten tribes would have endured, we do not know. I believe that there were among them and their descendants, many who remained believing and obedient to the Lord's commandments.

We do know that the lost ten tribes have continued to have their own prophets. They have not received all of the priesthood blessings there as have been available upon the earth in and from The Church of Jesus Christ of Latter-day Saints. We know this because, as has been quoted in this book, after they return, they will receive those blessings at the hands of Ephraim, which is through this Church and the Holy Priesthood that gives this Church its authority to administer the ordinances and covenants that are essential to eternal life with the Father and His Holy Son.

Chapter 14

SYNOPSIS OF
THE SECOND COMING AND THE LAST DAYS

In my recently-published book, *THE SECOND COMING AND THE LAST DAYS,* through more than 100 citations of scripture, visions and prophetic statements, I provided a time frame of events and times concerning the last days, leading up to the Second Coming of the Lord.

The next chapters of this book on the Return of the Lost Ten Tribes, it will be necessary to refer to that time frame and some of the events discussed in the book on the Second Coming. Rather than insert in this book more than one hundred twenty pages of that book, I will instead give a synopsis thereof, so the times, events and points about which I wish to write hereinafter can be better understood. In *The Second Coming and The Last Days*, we learn:

1 – The Children of Light—the righteous—can know of the times and seasons—which means appointed times of holidays and of prophesied events.

2 – How we know that the first six seals written about in the *Book of Revelation*, which mean the first six thousand years of the earth's mortal existence, have passed.

3 – We reviewed events John the Revelator saw happening during the Seventh Seal—the seventh thousand years; and specifically, that would happen after the start of the Seventh Seal, but before the Lord's Second Coming. John sees wars, plagues and great tribulations, especially during the last seven years before His Second Coming.

4 - Calculations are made as to the time frame from the start of the seventh seal until the start of the three-and-a-half year war of Armageddon. More is also explained of how and when certain events will take place.

5 – In Daniel's vision, he saw the abomination that makes desolate, which would occur twice, both focused on the temple(s), once one hundred sixty-seven years before Christ's birth, and another just before the Lord's Second Coming. King Antiochus defiled the temple in Jerusalem by sacrificing pigs—the most unclean of all beasts in Jewish culture—on the altar, and then forcing the Levite priests to eat the meat thereof. There had been twice-daily offerings in that temple, which offerings ceased, for an extended period of time. I believe that the prophesied second occurrence has been/is currently being fulfilled.

Before proceeding to the second occurrence of the abomination that makes desolate, I will define the two words: "Abomination" means, among other things, "vile, vicious, or horrible." "Desolate" means, among other things, "uninhabited, unfrequented, deserted of people, in a state of bleak and dismal emptiness."

Beginning in early 2020, the vicious and horrible Covid-19 virus, more accurately referred to as the CCP virus—Chinese Communist Party virus—began to ravage the world, killing, by the end of June, more than 500,000 people, and infecting over ten million—counting only reported cases, which may exclude millions of deaths in China and other dictatorships, who routinely give false information. That abomination, the virus, fits the word's definition—vile, vicious or horrible.

In March 2020, The Church of Jesus Christ of Latter-day Saints closed all 168 of its operating temples throughout the world, in order to protect people from the vicious virus, and to be a good global citizen. The temples, for at least a period of time have since been, and will continue to be, closed to the performance of normal, multiple sacred ordinances therein. These closures leave those temples—not just one, at this time—deserted of people, unfrequented, and bleakly and dismally empty. To frequent temple goers, this has become a bleak and dismal time of being unable to enter there and have the rich spiritual experience of participating in those sacred ordinances in behalf of our ancestors.

6 – Other prophecies of the last days and the second coming from The Old Testament, The New Testament, The Doctrine and Covenants and The Book of Mormon—Another Testament of Jesus Christ, are quoted and discussed.

7 - The three appearances of the Savior that all form part of His Second Coming are explained.

8 – The fulfillment of other prophecies is detailed.

9 – The two witnesses—also called "olive trees" and "candlesticks"—and their power used to defend Israel against the armies of other nations of the world are discussed.

10 – There follow prophecies and relevant statements from modern-day prophets, apostles, and other Church authorities, including from: Joseph Smith, Brigham Young, John Taylor, Wilford Woodruff, George Albert Smith, Orson Pratt, Charles W. Penrose, Spencer W. Kimball, George A. Cannon, Ezra Taft Benson, Boyd K. Packer, Gordon B. Hinckley, Bruce R. McConkie, Vaughn J. Featherstone and Parley P. Pratt.

11 – Most of those prophecies and statements refer to the destruction of many of the major cities and states of the United States, and the collapse of the U. S. government.

12 – There is even the vision given to George Washington at Valley Forge, which showed him the destiny of the United States.

13 – A short instruction on how to prepare physically for what is to come.

14 – Another short instruction on how to prepare spiritually for what is to come.

In conclusion, the book *The Second Coming and The Last Days* explains much of what has happened, and will yet happen, before the Lord's Second Coming in power and great glory, which may well be as soon as in the year 2024.

Between now and then, much has to occur, and much destruction—of cities, states, countries and people—must come to pass.

In this book, *Return of the Lost Ten Tribes and Building Two Temples*, we have reviewed the prologue of our current time—July 2020. In chapters to follow, we will examine some of the significant events that are yet to come.

Chapter 15

POSSIBLE SCENARIOS:

FOR WARS AND PLAGUES AND DESTRUCTION OF THE WICKED

In the chapters herein above we have read scriptural and prophetic statements about the events to occur, the gathering and restoration—return—of the lost ten tribes, the wars that will take place, and the building of two temples—all before the second coming of the Lord with power and great glory.

In my book *The Second Coming and The Last Days,* I presented scriptural and prophetic statements about the last days and the Lord's second coming, with many dates and times explained so the reader may have a better understanding of both the events that are to occur and a basic time frame for the fulfillment of the needed and prophesied events. I will not repeat all of those things here.

However, let me offer a short list of events that will be necessary to occur, potentially within the next four years—with a possible additional time of a couple of years for completion. After making that list, we will look at possible scenarios for all of the events listed to take place, or be completed, in time before Christ's great second coming.

Why is it necessary to list and discuss possible scenarios, rather than simply quote and review what the scriptures and prophetic utterances have told us? The answer is simple—neither the scriptures nor statements of prophets have provided the exact times, means or other relevant information that fill in those blanks.

We have already read in this book the information available concerning those events where precise place and time frame are not foretold. Prophecies give much insight and detail. But they also leave out information that is, and would be necessary, to list and provide the exact details, times, places and means for all of the listed events to occur. So, I cannot say, with certainty, exactly how and when each event will happen. But I can state what must, and will need to, be completed, before the Lord's second coming.

I will provide "possible scenarios" based upon scriptures and prophecies quoted herein, together with inspiration and impressions that have come, concerning the fulfillment of those time and events where unanswered blanks remain.

As I have stated before, I am not a prophet of God. I will, nonetheless, provide information that could fill in what the prophets have left blank about the times and events addressed herein.

These possible scenarios are very plausible. But the Lord may fulfill His words and prophecies in different and unexpected ways.

The Lord often does exactly that. When most people read a vision or prophecy, whether in scripture, or from the mouth or pen of a living prophet, those individuals may look forward to the fulfillment thereof in a certain way or at a certain time. The vision or prophecy always comes to pass, but often at a time, and/or in a way, that was not foreseeable to virtually anyone when it was spoken or written. Such could be the case with any number, or even all, of the possible scenarios we will herein consider.

A good example of this circumstance is that about which I wrote in Chapter 14 herein above concerning the fulfilling of the second occurrence of the abomination that makes desolate. Having read of how the first occurrence took place, virtually no one, if not exactly no one, expected the second occurrence in the last days to happen as it has.

Using the time frame and information concerning the Seventh (7th) Seal, or the seventh thousand years of the earth's mortal existence, I will use, without further explanation, the time frame and events of which I wrote in *The Second Coming and The Last Days* to place the time and events in the following possible scenarios.

We know that the end of the last three-and-a-half years before the second of the three major appearances of the Lord that are part of His Second Coming occurs when He plants His foot on the Mount of Olives to provide an escape route for the surviving part of the Israeli army. The start of that forty-two-month war will be at the end of the approximate twenty and 83/100 (20.83) years after April 6, 2000, as explained in *The Second Coming and The Last Days*.

To give only a brief and short review of the time frame, the chapter headings of both chapters eight and nine of the Book of Revelation, inform us that John the Revelator sees "fire and desolation" (in chapter 8), and "also sees the wars and plagues" (in chapter 9), "poured out **during the seventh seal and before the Lord comes**".

So, the seventh seal—the seventh thousand years—began in April 2000. Twenty and 83/100 years thereafter would be February 3, 2021, give or take twelve or thirteen days. If the counting were to start on January 1, 2000, then the 0.83 year would end on October 29, 2020, give or take twelve or thirteen days.

Starting on a date within the above paragraph's range, there are numerous events that must take place, or be completed before the Lord's second coming.

Revelation Chapter 9 details the wars and plagues that John saw.

He saw smoke coming from a pit. This could well be symbolic of destruction brought about by Satan—or by one of more of his major followers who possessed great political and military power. These could certainly include brutal and evil dictator(s) in one or more of certain of today's nations. The obvious two start with "C" and "R".

I will here print verses 2-3 and 7-11, after which I will discuss those verses from Revelation Chapter 9.

> 2 And he opened the bottomless pit; and there arose a smoke out of the pit, as the smoke of a great furnace; and the sun and the air were darkened by reason of the smoke of the pit.
> 3 And there came out of the smoke locusts upon the earth: and unto them was given power, as the scorpions of the earth have power.
>
> 7 And the shapes of the locusts *were* like unto horses prepared unto battle; and on their heads *were* as it were crowns like gold, and their faces *were* as the faces of men.
> 8 And they had hair as the hair of women, and their teeth were as *the teeth* of lions.
> 9 And they had breastplates, as it were breastplates of iron; and the sound of their wings *was* as the sound of chariots of many horses running to battle.
> 10 And they had tails like unto scorpions, and there were stings in their tails: and their power *was* to hurt men five months.
> 11 And they had a king over them, *which is* the angel of the bottomless pit, whose name in the Hebrew tongue *is* Abaddon, but in the Greek tongue hath *his* name Apollyon.[93]

The smoke could be from nuclear weapons. Out of the smoke came locusts upon the earth who received power. Locusts could be used to describe John's seeing hordes of fighters advancing to battle. Verse 7 describes their shapes and appearance. John, sees modern-day weaponry from his vantage point of the first century after the birth of Jesus Christ. (See Revelation 9: 2-3.)

"Horses prepared unto battle" with golden crowns on their heads and faces like that of men, could be his way of describing tanks, helicopters, jet fighters, armored personnel carriers etc. (See Revelation 9: 7.)

These locusts had hair—perhaps covering(s) and/or camouflage, and teeth as of lions. Both "teeth of Lions" and "hair" symbolize strength, virility and power. (See Revelation 9: 8.)

They had breastplates as of iron—as tanks, armor-covered military transports or other such vehicles have. They had wings with "the sound of chariots of many horses running to battle. That could again seek to describe helicopters and jet fighters, both of which have wings. Tanks and armored carriers, although not having wings, can move rapidly. In scriptures, wings are used to describe the ability to fly or move, to move fast, and to have great power. (See Revelation 9: 9.)

These war-making locusts had tails like scorpions with stings in their tails. Again, a tank would be the weapon that would look most like a scorpion that has a tail. The stings could well describe the bullets and other projectiles that are fired from tanks and other armored vehicles. (See Revelation 9: 10.)

This army of "locusts" had a leader—king—over them, who is either Satan or one of his chief evil mortal leaders at that—this—time on earth.

Next, verses 14 through 19 tell of a war or plague that lasts ". . . an hour, and a day, and a month, and a year," during which time a third part of men will be slain. These verses follow:

> 14 Saying to the sixth angel which had the trumpet, Loose the four angels which are bound in the great river Euphrates.
> 15 And the four angels were loosed, which were prepared for an hour, and a day, and a month, and a year, for to slay the third part of men.
> 16 And the number of the army of the horsemen *were* two hundred thousand thousand: and I heard the number of them.
> 17 And thus I saw the horses in the vision, and them that sat on them, having breastplates of fire, and of jacinth, and brimstone: and the heads of the horses *were* as the heads of lions; and out of their mouths issued fire and smoke and brimstone.
> 18 By these three was the third part of men killed, by the fire, and by the smoke, and by the brimstone, which issued out of their mouths.
> 19 For their power is in their mouth, and in their tails: for their tails *were* like unto serpents, and had heads, and with them they do hurt.
> 20 And the rest of the men which were not killed by these plagues yet repented not of the works of their hands, that they should not worship devils, and idols of gold, and silver, and brass, and stone, and of wood: which neither can see, nor hear, nor walk:
> 21 Neither repented they of their murders, nor of their sorceries, nor of their fornication, nor of their thefts.[94]

Having already stated what is given in verses 14 and 15, we will go to verse 16, which tells us that the army involved in this war (and perhaps another war written about in Revelation as well) is to have two hundred million soldiers! That is an army the size of which has never been known on the earth.

Verse 17 refers to the horses on which these soldiers ride. Obviously, they are not actual horses, but in John's time frame, whatever carried them would be compared to, or symbolized by, horses, for they then had no engine-powered means of transportation. John further tells us that the heads of these "horses" "were as the heads of lions; and out of their mouths issued fire and smoke and brimstone."

Let us analyze each of those items:

"Head of lions" symbolizes courage, power, strength, domination, as well as other such characteristics.

"Fire issuing out of their mouths" could certainly describe how modern-day weaponry, such as tanks, helicopters and jets would propel their projectiles and missiles out of their barrels and cannons, etc.

"Smoke and brimstone" would describe the smoke that issues out of the barrel of the tank, etc., upon firing the explosive shell, which then produces an explosion of brimstone-like result as it strikes the target.

Verse 18 tells us the number of men killed by this/these army(ies)—the third part of men. This could be interpreted to mean literally one third of all men in the world, or more likely, a third of the men in the armies, or in the area in which the war or a specific battle is being fought, or only that part of the war/battle that John saw.

Verse 19 explains where their power is. Power, in this case, would refer to the power to harm or destroy. It is both in their mouth and tails. Picture a tank with its main barrel able to swivel, but generally putting forward. Thus, the barrel of the tank's cannon is at its mouth.

Below the main cannon barrel on a tank are multiple machine guns, that generally can also swivel, and are pointed to the rear—its tail—and can be turned to both sides.

Verse 20 makes at least two main points about the men who are not killed. The cause of death is referred to as "these plagues." It is interesting that it is not "weapons", "horses" or "war" used to refer to what brought about their deaths.

Perhaps John uses "plagues" because this would be in keeping with his use of "locusts" in verse 3 of this chapter. It could also be that some of the weapons being used could contain poison or chemical gases, and/or radiation. Any of these types of weapons would result in what throughout history has generally been referred to as "plagues."

The second main point of verse 20 is that those men who were not killed do not repent of their wicked or evil ways. They continue to worship wealth, power and idol gods. These false gods are not like the Lord. He can see, hear and walk. The false gods can do none of those things. In fact, they cannot do anything—except lead people away from the true Lord God, Jesus Christ.

Finally, for chapter 9, verse 21 tells us that those who survive have not repented of any of their other sins of various types.

Note, many believe that this "thirteen-month war" will take place on United States' soil. Having such an extended land mass on which fighting and bombing could occur, it would be easy to see that tanks and other armored military vehicles, helicopters and jet fighters could all be involved. Their missiles could inflict destruction and death for great distances.

Chapter 16 of the Book of Revelation tells us of plagues poured out upon the wicked. Then, it instructs us of the great Battle, or War, of Armageddon. In this chapter of this book, we will only list the plagues, because we will later deal in greater detail with the War of Armageddon.

The seven angels are directed to "pour out the vials of the wrath of God upon the earth," in verse 1. The angels proceed to do so.

This pouring out of plagues upon the wicked of the earth is part of God's mercy for the righteous and good, who look to Him as their God. They are to save the good and to sweep great hosts of men from the earth—to cleanse the earth preparatory to the coming of the Lord.

Vial—plague—1 causes "a noisome and grievous sore upon the men which had the mark of the beast, and upon them which worshipped his image; (See verse 2). This could well be the plague Zechariah speaks of in 14:12:

> And this shall be the plague wherewith the LORD will smite all the people that have fought against Jerusalem; Their flesh shall consume away while they stand upon their feet, and their eyes shall consume away in their holes, and their tongue shall consume away in their mouth.[95]

The Lord could send a plague of His own making, or this could be a man-made plague that the Lord directs to sweep away the wicked. Its source could be radiation, or chemical and/or biological weapons.

Vial—plague—2 is "poured upon the sea, and it became as the blood of a dead man: and every living soul died in the sea;" (See verse 3). In The Doctrine and Covenants, the Lord tells of the curse that shall come upon the waters in the last days:

> Behold, I, the Lord, in the beginning blessed the waters; but in the last days, by the mouth of my servant John, I cursed the waters.
> Wherefore, the days will come that no flesh shall be safe upon the waters.[96]

This danger on the waters could also come from contamination, whether by nuclear radiation, chemical or biological weapons.

Vial—plague—3, similar to Vial 2, is poured "upon the rivers and fountains of waters; and they became blood;" (See verse 4). The same analysis of the second plague can apply to this third plague on rivers and fountains of waters.

Vial—plague—4 is poured out upon the sun, and the angel received power to "scorch men with fire;" (See verses 8-9). Since this power is used on the wicked, it seems unlikely that it is just a universal climate change effect. It will be something that is intended to clear away the wicked.

Vial—plague—5 is poured upon the seat of the beast—the place, city or otherwise where he is based, and where he exercises his authority—and his kingdom becomes full of darkness and pain; (See verses 10-11). Again, this plague is aimed at the devil and his evil leaders and their followers.

Vial—plague—6 is poured out "upon the great river Euphrates; and the water thereof was dried up . . . ;" (See verses 12-14). As the evil leader(s) of the devil on the earth prepare for Armageddon, using "false miracles" to impress and motivate their wicked followers, the Lord begins to thwart their unrighteous efforts by drying up the great Euphrates. Symbolically, Euphrates can signify the pleasure arising from love of self and the falsity of the reasoning of the wicked.

Vial—plague—7 comes after Satan and his beast, work miracles (amazing things) to gather the "kings of the earth and the whole world" to battle God Almighty; (See verses 15-21).

We read that he who watches and keeps his sacred garments shall be blessed—a reference to temples.

Satan gathers his wicked and evil followers—which are numerous—into Armageddon.

The 7th plague is poured out "into the air; and there came a great voice out of the temple of heaven, from the throne, saying, It is done;" (See verse 17).

So, what is the 7th plague? First of all, it is immediately preceded by, or is brought on by, "a great earthquake, such as was not since men were upon the earth, so mighty an earthquake, and so great." (See verse 18.)

I want to quote verses 17 through 20 of this chapter 16 of Revelation, for I am going to compare what they say with another prophecy that speaks of the restoration of the lost ten tribes.

> 17 And the seventh angel poured out his vial into the air; and there came a great voice out of the temple of heaven, from the throne, saying, It is done.
> 18 And there were voices, and thunders, and lightnings; **and there was a great earthquake, such as was not since men were upon the earth, so mighty an earthquake, *and* so great.**
> 19 And the great city was divided into three parts, and the cities of the nations fell: and great Babylon came in remembrance before God, to give unto her the cup of the wine of the fierceness of his wrath.
> 20 And every island fled away, and the mountains were not found[97] (Emphasis added.)

You have already read in Chapter 13 of this book the revelation found in The Doctrine and Covenants that speaks of Christ ending the War of Armageddon when He plants His foot upon the Mount of Olives and it cleaves in two. At that time the following occurs:

> 18 When the Lamb shall stand upon Mount Zion, and with him a hundred and forty-four thousand, having his Father's name written on their foreheads.
> 19 Wherefore, prepare ye for the coming of the Bridegroom; go ye, go ye out to meet him.
> 20 For behold, he shall stand upon the mount of Olivet, and upon the mighty ocean, even the great

> deep, and upon the islands of the sea, and upon the land of Zion.
>
> 21 And he shall utter his voice out of Zion, and **he shall speak from Jerusalem, and his voice shall be heard among all people**;
>
> 22 And it shall be a voice as the voice of many waters, and as **the voice of a great thunder, which shall break down the mountains, and the valleys shall not be found.**
>
> 23 He shall command the great deep, and it shall be driven back into the north countries, **and the islands shall become one land;**[98]

Apparently, that great earthquake shall accomplish multiple things: 1 - open the way for the Jews—in the trapped and depleted Israeli army—to escape from the immense army seeking to destroy them; 2 - open the way for the return of the lost ten tribes from the "northern countries;" 3 - kill many of the wicked in the world; 4 - bring with it great talent-heavy hailstones; and 5 - break down the mountains, exalt the valleys and bring portions of the earth's land back together as before the land of the earth was divided.

In addition to comparing this great earthquake to an earthquake-causing event concerning the lost ten tribes, it is worth noting the effects of the great earthquake when Christ plants His foot on the Mount of Olives.

Jerusalem is divided into three parts. Other cities of the nations fall. And the Lord delivers to Babylon—which stands for the world (See The Doctrine and Covenants 1:16,) the fierceness of His wrath for the world's wickedness and evil.

Now, let us read the last verse of this chapter 16 of Revelation. It is here that the 7th plague is explained.

> And there fell upon men a great hail out of heaven, *every stone* about the weight of a talent: and men blasphemed God because of the **plague of the**

hail; for the **plague thereof** was exceeding great.[99] (Emphasis added.)

So, the 7th plague is impressive indeed. It is possible that it could be said to include the great earthquake, and the hail. It could also be only the hail, as the above verse states. This great hail has hailstones about the weight of a talent. Exodus 38:25, 26 tell us that a talent is equivalent to 50 shekels, or 75.6 pounds in weight!

With such ponderous hail falling upon wicked and evil men, is it any wonder that they blasphemed God. I do not say they are justified under any circumstances to blaspheme God. But, those who do not reverence the true God in the first place, would surely be more than angry having such stones falling upon them.

SUMMARY OF POTENTIAL DESTRUCTION OF THE WICKED AND EVIL

Let us summarize the potential impacts upon the earth and the destruction of the wicked and evil by multiple forces that could all occur at once, or over a period of time. The list and destructive capacity of all the forces named below would be astonishing and devastating.

1 – Thousands and thousands of jet fighters, helicopters, cruise and other missiles, tanks and other military vehicles.

2 – Two hundred million soldiers with their rifles, hand grenades, drones, mortars.

3 – Atomic bombs and hydrogen bombs and other explosive and radiation-producing weapons.

4 – The armies of both the **lost ten tribes** with their potential of millions who are armed with possibly even very advanced weapons, coupled with the **remnant of the seed of Joseph** who will be like "a young lion among the flocks of sheep."[100] Both of these groups will fight those who oppose the Lord's people. They, not the wicked, shall triumph.

Last, but not least, before describing number 5 of the destructive forces, let me take us back to the New World of the Americas at the time of the crucifixion of the Savior. We will here read of the great destruction that came to the wicked there. We will first read the chapter heading, followed by some of the verses from Chapter 8 of the Book of Third Nephi:

Tempests, earthquakes, fires, whirlwinds, and physical upheavals attest the crucifixion of Christ—Many people are destroyed—Darkness covers the land for three days—Those who remain bemoan their fate. About A.D. 33–34.

5 And it came to pass in the thirty and fourth year, . . . there arose a **great storm, such an one as never had been known in all the land**.

6 And there was also a **great and terrible tempest**; and there was terrible thunder, insomuch that **it did shake the whole earth as if it was about to divide asunder**.

7 And there were exceedingly sharp lightnings, such as never had been known in all the land.

8 And the **city of Zarahemla did take fire**.

9 And the **city of Moroni did sink into the depths of the sea, and the inhabitants thereof were drowned**.

10 And the **earth was carried up upon the city of Moronihah**, that in the place of the city there became a great mountain.

11 And there was a **great and terrible destruction in the land southward**.

12 But behold, there was a **more great and terrible destruction in the land northward**; for behold, the **whole face of the land was change**d, because of the tempest and the whirlwinds, and the thunderings and the lightnings, and the **exceedingly great quaking of the whole earth**;

13 And the **highways were broken up**, and the **level roads were spoiled**, and **many smooth places became rough**.

14 And **many great and notable cities were sunk**, and **many were burned**, and **many were shaken till the buildings thereof had fallen to the earth**, and the **inhabitants thereof were slain**, and the **places were left desolate**.

15 And there were some cities which remained; but the **damage thereof was exceedingly great**, and there were **many in them who were slain**.

16 And there were **some who were carried away in the whirlwind**; and whither they went no man knoweth, save they know that they were carried away.

17 And thus the **face of the whole earth became deformed**, because of the tempests, and the thunderings, and the lightnings, and the quaking of the earth.

18 And behold, the rocks were rent in twain; they were broken up upon the face of the whole earth, insomuch that they were found in broken fragments, and in seams and in cracks, upon all the face of the land.

19 And it came to pass that when the thunderings, and the lightnings, and the storm, and the tempest, and the quakings of the earth did cease—for behold, **they did last for about the space of three hours**; . . . and then behold, there was **darkness upon the face of the land**.[101] (Emphasis added.)

We see in the above chapter heading and verses the astonishingly great destruction and death that came upon the land and the people in the Western Hemisphere at the time of Jesus Christ's crucifixion. A large portion of the population there was killed. But, there were many who were spared alive. The Lord's explains why:

> 10 . . . [Multiple cities] have I caused to be burned with fire, and the inhabitants thereof, **because of their wickedness in casting out the prophets, and stoning those whom I did send to declare unto them concerning their wickedness and their abominations.**
>
> 11 And because they did cast them all out, that there were none righteous among them, I did send down fire and destroy them, that their wickedness and abominations might be hid from before my face, that the blood of the prophets and the saints whom I sent among them might not cry unto me from the ground against them.
>
> 12 And many great destructions have I caused to come upon this land, and upon this people, **because of their wickedness and their abominations**.
>
> 13 O all ye that are **spared because ye were more righteous than they**, will ye not now return unto me, and repent of your sins, and be converted, that I may heal you?
>
> 14 Yea, verily I say unto you, if ye will come unto me ye shall have eternal life. Behold, mine arm of mercy is extended towards you, and whosoever will come, him will I receive; and blessed are those who come unto me.[102] (Emphasis added.)

We read that the only people spared were those who "were more righteous than they [who were destroyed]. So, the Lord was able to destroy the wicked, but spare the more righteous. We know that He can do whatever He wants or needs to do. How, exactly, he brought it about, we do not know. We only know that He did so and can do it again.

Such an event of sifting the grain from the chaff—among people on Earth—is not only found, as we have just read in Third Nephi. We have the example of Noah and his family. Of all the people on Earth, only eight souls, Noah, his wife, his three sons and their wives, were spared. All others died in the flood.

Now we will read when it shall hereafter also occur.

> 35 Heaven and earth shall pass away, but my words shall not pass away.
> 36 ¶ But of that day and hour knoweth no *man*, no, not the angels of heaven, but my Father only.
> 37 But as the days of Noe *were,* so shall also the coming of the Son of man be.
> 38 For as in the days that were before the flood they were eating and drinking, marrying and giving in marriage, until the day that Noe entered into the ark,
> 39 And knew not until the flood came, and took them all away; so shall also the coming of the Son of man be.
> 40 **Then shall two be in the field; the one shall be taken, and the other left.**
> 41 **Two *women shall be* grinding at the mill; the one shall be taken, and the other left.**[103]

(Emphasis added.)

As I wrote above, we do not know how the Lord can or has done this, or how He will hereafter repeat it. We only know that He can and will do so.

When the Lord comes again, He will have an earth populated by good and honorable people. The dross of the earth will be gone.

Now, knowing that by whatever means necessary, the Lord will clear out the wicked and evil on the earth, prior to, and/or at the time of His Second Coming, we will discuss some of the remaining means He could use.

5 – We have read of earthquakes occurring. We will put some ideas together as we consider these.

A – We know that when Christ shall plant His foot on the Mount of Olives, at or near the end of the three-and-a-half-year War of Armageddon, there shall be "so mighty" an earthquake, and so great." We shall read from three verses of the Book of Revelation:

18 . . . and there was a **great earthquake**, such as was not since men were upon the earth, so mighty an earthquake, *and* so great.
19 And the great city was divided into three parts, and the cities of the nations fell: and great Babylon came in remembrance before God, to give unto her the cup of the wine of the fierceness of his wrath.
20 And **every island fled away, and the mountains were not found**.
21 And there fell upon men a great hail out of heaven, *every stone* about the weight of a talent: and men blasphemed God because of the plague of the hail; for the plague thereof was exceeding great.[104] (Emphasis added.)

Let us note several things about this earthquake:

It will be a great one. Islands shall flee and mountains shall not be found—islands and mountains shall cease to exist.

Seventy-five-pound hailstones shall fall upon, and kill wicked men.

B – We have herein read that after the two witnesses are killed by the armies opposed to Israel, they lie in the street. After three-and-one-half days, they "ascended up to heaven in a cloud; and their enemies beheld them."

Verse 13 of Revelation Chapter 11 then states: "And the same hour was there a **great earthquake**. . ." (Emphasis added.)

So again, there is a great earthquake. But, we are not yet done!

C – We have previously read about the return of the lost ten tribes of Israel. We will review some, and then continue our list of events that will wipe out the wicked.

Remember the inspired song by Eliza R. Snow, written after she listened to the Prophet Joseph Smith speak of the location of the lost ten tribes. I quote in pertinent part:

> "And when the Lord saw fit to hide the Ten
>   Lost Tribes away,
> Thou, earth, wast severed to provide an orb on
>   which they stay."[105]

We previously read the account from the Journal of Wilford Woodruff of a prophetic statement by Brigham Young:

> . . . the ten tribes of Israel are on a portion of the earth—a portion separated from the main land.[106]

Remember the Allegory of the tame and wild olive trees. After planting in the poorest spot in the vineyard—the world—the Lord then planted in a place poorer than the first. That can only be outside of this world.

I will again quote, this time a part of, the prophetic answer(s) given by the Apostle Parley P. Pratt:

> The stars, which will fall to the earth, are fragments, which have been broken off from the earth from time to time, in the mighty convulsions of nature. Some in the days of Enoch, some perhaps in the days of Peleg, some with the ten tribes, and some at the crucifixion of the Messiah. These all must be restored again at the "times of restitution of ALL THINGS." **This will restore the ten tribes of Israel; and also bring again Zion, even Enoch's city.** It will bring back the tree of life, which is in the midst of the paradise of God; that you and I may partake of it. [See Rev.11, 7.] **When these fragments (some of which are vastly larger than the present earth) are brought back and joined to this earth, it will cause a convulsion of all nature, the graves of the Saints will be opened, and they rise from the dead; while the mountains will flow down, the valleys rise, the sea retire to its own place, the islands and continents will be removed, and earth be rolled together as a scroll. . . .**[107]

Finally, I will again quote in pertinent part what Eliza R. Snow heard the Prophet Joseph say:

> . . . that when the 10 tribes were taken away, the Lord cut the earth in two, Joseph striking his left hand in the center with the edge of his right to illustrate the idea, and that they (the 10 tribes) were on an orb or planet by themselves, and when they returned with the portion of this earth that was taken away with them, the coming together of these two bodies or orbs would cause a shock and make the "earth reel to and fro like a drunken man."[108]

With all of these reminders from prior pages of this book, we now have an immense earthquake—convulsions of all nature on the earth that will inevitably result from the return of the orb, or fragment, and/or fragments, of the earth, as it, or they, reconnect(s) with the earth.

Before continuing to the next similar contributor to the destruction of the wicked, we will consider the typical environmental effects of the impact of even a relatively small meteor colliding with the earth. As it strikes land, there is an immense amount of dust and other debris that shoot up into the earth's atmosphere. This could cause darkness to cover the earth, which would black-out the sun, moon and stars. Huge shock waves reverberate around the world. Heat radiation follows, and tsunamis could develop. As with most earthquakes of even a far lesser magnitude, aftershocks would almost certainly follow.

Remember also, one verse concerning the return of the lost ten tribes, found in The Doctrine and Covenants Section 133:28.

Referring to the said ten tribes' return, we read:

Their enemies shall become a prey unto them,[109]

Therefore, even after the destructive effects of the earthquake their return will certainly cause, any enemies that may remain will become their prey. That could be from the environmental effects specified above, and/or from subsequent battles fought.

D. Now I will address the fourth possible—likely—cause of earthquake in the last days. That is the return from heaven of Enoch's City of Zion to the New Jerusalem. When that portion of the earth returns to, and connects with, the earth, it would certainly seem likely that another earthquake would occur.

E. Let us now review as much as is possible the chronological order of the above four (4) earthquakes. We know that the City of Enoch must return prior to the Lord's great Second Coming. After the return of Enoch's city and people, they will participate in the building of the city of Zion, the New Jerusalem. So, this will likely be earlier than the earthquake at the time Christ plants His foot on the Mount of Olives, which causes another earthquake.

F. The Prophet Joseph Smith has previously been quoted herein stating that the restoration of the lost ten tribes must take place before the Lord's Second Coming. Furthermore, they will participate in the rebuilding of Old Jerusalem and the temple there.

G. The earthquake at the time the two witnesses are called up to heaven in a cloud could be at the same time as, or before, the Lord planting his foot on the Mount of Olives.

H. The second of the three major appearances of the Lord in the process of His Second Coming will be when he plants His foot on the Mount of Olives. As written above, this appearance and event could occur either at the same time as, or after the earthquake that takes place when the two witnesses are called up to heaven.

The significant events listed above, together with the Lord simply taking some in whirlwinds or by other means, could clearly—obviously will—bring about the destruction of the wicked and evil people on the earth. This will occur before the Second Coming of the Lord with power and great glory. Why? He will not show Himself on Earth to the wicked or evil. When He comes in His third major appearance in His Second Coming, it will be to an earth that has been cleansed from the horrible wickedness and evil that exist today, and which will almost certainly be worse hereafter, just prior to His great coming.

Chapter 16

TEMPLES

Prior to discussing the building of these two temples, let us consider the purpose for which temples are now built by The Church of Jesus Christ of Latter-day Saints. The purpose is to allow its members to receive—first for themselves, and then in behalf of their kindred dead—the ordinances, and to make the covenants necessary to obtain—with and through the grace of Jesus Christ's atoning sacrifice—eternal life and exaltation with Christ and the Father.

Therefore, it will be in the two temples—in Old Jerusalem and in New Jerusalem--that so many of the children of Israel, from all twelve tribes, will be able to make those covenants and receive those essential ordinances for their own eternal salvation, and for their ancestors.

The prophet Malachi, who lived long after Elijah, following the Babylonian captivity, stated:

> Behold, I will send you Elijah the prophet before the coming of the great and dreadful day of the Lord:
> And he shall turn the heart of the fathers to the children, and the heart of the children to their fathers, lest I come and smite the earth with a curse.[110]

Elijah held the keys to the sealing power, by which he could seal the heavens, as well as, by which husbands and wives are sealed together, and their children are sealed to them, their parents, for time and for all eternity. He used that power during one part of his life on Earth, to seal the heavens, stopping all dew and rain from falling. Let us also read of some other interesting facts about him.

The great prophet Elijah spoke to Ahab, the seventh king of Israel after Jeroboam I, and said:

> As the Lord God of Israel liveth, before whom I stand, there shall not be dew nor rain these years, but according to my word.[111]

And thus, the heavens were sealed at Elijah's word. Elijah, at the Lord's command, hid in the cavity of a rock near to a brook of water, where he was fed by the ravens. His sealing of the heavens came to affect Elijah, as well as the rest of Israel, for the brook dried up.

The Lord directed him to go to Zarephath, where the Lord had commanded a widow to sustain him. He met the widow gathering sticks as he came to the gate of the city. Elijah called to her to bring him a little water in a vessel. Then, as she was going to fetch it, he called out again, saying, "Bring me, I pray thee, a morsel of bread in thine hand. The rest of the story is interesting:

> 12 And she said, *As* the LORD thy God liveth, I have not a cake, but an handful of meal in a barrel, and a little oil in a cruse: and, behold, I *am* gathering two sticks, that I may go in and dress it for me and my son, that we may eat it, and die.
> 13 And Elijah said unto her, Fear not; go *and* do as thou hast said: but make me thereof a little cake first, and bring *it* unto me, and after make for thee and for thy son.
> 14 For thus saith the LORD God of Israel, The barrel of meal shall not waste, neither shall the cruse of oil fail, until the day *that* the LORD sendeth rain

> upon the earth.
> 15 And she went and did according to the saying of Elijah: and she, and he, and her house, did eat *many* days.
> 16 *And* the barrel of meal wasted not, neither did the cruse of oil fail, according to the word of the LORD, which he spake by Elijah.[112]

You may remember how the story continues. The woman's son became seriously ill and died. Elijah "revived" the boy and took him to his mother, who said:

> ... Now by this I know that thou art a man of God, and that the word of the Lord in thy mouth is truth.[113]

The above story is prologue to the drama that was yet to occur. Elijah was unafraid to boldly speak the word of God to Ahab, the king. I will briefly recount the interesting story, in I Kings 18. I recommend you read it.

Elijah met Ahab, who said, "Art thou he that troubleth Israel?"

Elijah answered,

> I have not troubled Israel; but thou, and thy father's house, in that ye have forsaken the commandments of the Lord, and thou hast followed Baalim.
> Now therefore send, and gather to meall Israel unto mount Carmel, and the prophets of Baal four hundred and fifty, and the prophets of the groves four hundred, which eat at Jezebel's table.[114]

Ahab did so. Elijah told the people that they should follow the true God. He called for two bullocks, for the priests to choose one, cut it in pieces, lay it on wood and put **no** fire under. Then they should call on their gods to burn the offering. They did so from morning until noon. At noon, Elijah mocked them, for nothing came from their cries to their phony gods. The priests cried aloud, cut themselves after their manner and prophesied until nearly the time for the evening sacrifice. Still nothing happened.

Then Elijah took twelve stones representing the tribes of the sons of Jacob, and repaired the altar of the Lord that was broken. He made a large trench around the altar, put on the altar wood and the pieces of his bullock.

Three times, Elijah told people to fill four barrels with water and pour it on the sacrifice and on the wood. Water ran around about the altar and filled the trench.

At the time of the evening sacrifice, Elijah called on the Lord God of Abraham, Isaac, and of Israel, asking that He let it be known that He is God in Israel.

> Then the fire of the Lord fell, and consumed the burnt sacrifice, and the wood, and the stones, and the dust, and licked up the water that was in the trench.
> And when all the people saw it, they fell on their faces; and they said, The Lord, he is the God; the Lord, he is the God.
> And Elijah said unto them, Take the prophets of Baal; let not one of them escape. And they took them: and Elijah brought them down to the brook Kishon, and slew them there.[115]

In the Book of Mormon, we read the account of the Savior's visit to the Nephite people, following His crucifixion and resurrection. During His visit there, he quoted the scripture from Malachi, quoted previously, about turning the heart of the fathers to the children, etc.

On September 21, 1823, the Angel Moroni quoted the same passage to Joseph Smith. Then, Joseph Smith again heard the very same scripture on November 3, 1831, as recorded in The Doctrine and Covenants 133:64.

So it should be obvious that before the Second Coming of the Lord, Jesus Christ, the Prophet Elijah would return to bestow the power that would bring about the turning of those hearts, as we just read.

That prophecy was in fact fulfilled on April 3, 1836, at the time of the dedication of the Kirtland Temple in Ohio. After the Lord had appeared, accepting the temple that had just been dedicated to Him, two prophets, Moses and Elias, appeared, one following the other. Earlier in this book, we read of what Moses did at the time of his appearance in the Kirtland Temple.

After Elias' appearance, Joseph records:

> 13 After this vision had closed, another great and glorious vision burst upon us; for Elijah the prophet, who was taken to heaven without tasting death, stood before us, and said:
> 14 Behold, the time has fully come, which was spoken of by the mouth of Malachi—testifying that he [Elijah] should be sent, before the great and dreadful day of the Lord come—
> 15 To turn the hearts of the fathers to the children, and the children to the fathers, lest the whole earth be smitten with a curse—[116]

It is interesting to contemplate that other people—namely, the Jews—have also long believed in the coming of Elijah "before the great and dreadful day of the Lord." The immense difference is that they still believe that the fulfillment of that prophecy is yet to come. In fact, orthodox Jews still look forward to Elijah's coming. At their holy feasts, they reserve an empty chair at the table for Elijah.

What members of The Church of Jesus Christ of Latter-day Saints understand is that Elijah has already come, and the priesthood keys he held were bestowed upon the Prophet Joseph Smith. Thereafter, Joseph bestowed them upon others, as he was commanded to do, so that those keys could endure to bless the lives of all mankind.

Just as Joel teaches of the great war in the land of Israel preceding the Second Coming, chapter 4 of the Book of Micah also prophecies (1) of the last days; (2) of the temple being built in the United States; (3) of people from many nations who shall come and say, "let us go up to the mountain of the Lord (His Temple) to be taught of His ways, (4) of Israel being gathered to its land, (5) of many nations being gathered against Israel—again reference to the battle, or war, of Armageddon; and (6) those opposing nations being defeated. Let's read only verses 1, 2, then 3 through 5, then 10, and finally, 11 through 13 from Micah:

> 1 BUT in the last days it shall come to pass, *that* **the mountain of the house of the LORD shall be established in the top of the mountains**, and it shall be exalted above the hills; and people shall flow unto it.
> 2 And many nations shall come, and say, Come, and let us go up to the mountain of the LORD, and to the house of the God of Jacob; and he will teach us of his ways, and we will walk in his paths: for the law shall go forth of Zion, and the word of the LORD from Jerusalem.[117]

Micah's statement of "the mountain of the house of the Lord" is nearly word-perfect with Isaiah's statement in his second chapter, verse 2: "the mountain of the Lord's house." No real difference. I have already stated that this refers to a temple of the Lord. This prophecy, by both Micah and Isaiah, has been fulfilled with the construction of the Lord's Temple in the mountain valley of Salt Lake City, Utah. We will continue in Micah:

> 3 ¶ And he shall judge among many people, and rebuke strong nations afar off; and they shall beat their swords into plowshares, and their spears into pruninghooks: nation shall not lift up a sword against nation, neither shall they learn war any more.
>
> 4 But they shall sit every man under his vine and under his fig tree; and none shall make *them* afraid: for the mouth of the LORD of hosts hath spoken *it*.
>
> 5 For all people will walk every one in the name of his god, and we will walk in the name of the LORD our God for ever and ever.[118]

Shortly before his death, the Prophet Joseph Smith stated the following about what had to take place before the Second Coming of the Savior would occur:

> Judah must return, Jerusalem must be rebuilt, and the temple, and water come out from under the temple, and the waters of the Dead Sea be healed. It will take some time to rebuild the walls of the city and the temple, etc., and all this must be done before the Son of Man will make His appearance.[119]

The walls of Jerusalem have been rebuilt. The promise is made that after the difficult labor of restoring the City of Jerusalem and the temple there, life will return to more normal and pleasant, and even that its citizens will be able to go into the cities of former enemies and be safe.

> 10 Be in pain, and labour to bring forth , O daughter of Zion, like a woman in travail: for now shalt thou go forth out of the city, and thou shalt dwell in the field, and thou shalt go *even* to Babylon; there shalt thou be delivered; there the LORD shall redeem thee from the hand of thine enemies.[120]

Zechariah speaks of building a temple as follows:

> 8 And I will bring them, and they shall dwell in the midst of Jerusalem: and they shall be my people, and I will be their God, in truth and in righteousness.
>
> 9 ¶ Thus saith the LORD of hosts; Let your hands be strong, ye that hear in these days these words by the mouth of the prophets, which *were* in the day *that* the foundation of the house of the LORD of hosts was laid, that the temple might be built.[121]

The Lord also states the following:

> 36 For it is ordained that in Zion, and in her stakes, and in Jerusalem, those places which I have appointed for refuge, shall be the places for your baptisms for your dead.
>
> 37 And again, verily I say unto you, how shall your washings be acceptable unto me, except ye perform them in a house which you have built to my name?[122]

It is in temples of The Church of Jesus Christ of Latter-day Saints that baptisms for the dead and washings acceptable to the Lord are performed.

Many Orthodox Jews, themselves, are talking about the construction of a third temple. Concerning this subject, an important scroll was discovered in the Middle East just a few years ago. Dr. Yigael Yadin of the Hebrew University is now translating this scroll, which he calls the Temple Scroll and concerning which he has said:

> The amazing thing about this scroll is that it was written as a Torah—a law— given by God to Moses. The entire text is written *in the first person singular, with God as the speaker.* Every other scroll from the Dead Sea is either a copy of an existent Biblical book or a Biblical commentary or a sectarian document

> composed by the Qumran community. Here we have for the first time a scroll that was apparently meant to be in the Biblical text but which was never part of the Biblical canon, so far as we know.[123]

(Italics added.)

With what does that text deal? Dr. Yadin says that it has the plans for the construction of a great temple and that it introduces a new feature into the temple. There are three courts instead of two, each exactly square. The middle and the outer courts of the temple are to have twelve gates, three on each side, and each gate is to be named for one of the Twelve Tribes of Israel. Dr. Yadin adds:

> This is significant. The whole apocalyptic literature and that of Qumran were occupied with the concept of uniting the twelve tribes of Israel as ordained by God. Here, too, the emphasis is on the twelve tribes, as it is so frequently also in the New Testament.[124]

Orson Pratt described another notable feature about the temple to be built in Jerusalem during the last days:

> **The Temple at Jerusalem will undoubtedly be built, by those who believe in the true Messiah.** Its construction will be, in some respects different from the Temples now being built. It will contain the throne of the Lord, upon which he will, at times, personally sit, and will reign over the house of Israel for ever.[125] (Emphasis added.)

Chapter 17

POSSIBLE SCENARIOS:

BUILDING THE TEMPLE IN OLD JERUSALEM

INTRODUCTION TO CHAPTER

This chapter is not intended to be based wholly upon revelation, prophecies or other known facts.

As I have stated elsewhere in this book, I am not a prophet of God. I am open to inspiration and impressions from the Spirit, but I declare that unless I state otherwise, or I am speaking of historical facts, I will present in this chapter "possible scenarios"—possibilities—as to the location for the rebuilding of the third Old Jerusalem Temple, and of the time frame in which it will be built.

I do know, based upon prophecies of modern-day prophets, that there will be built a temple there, before the Second Coming of the Savior, Jesus Christ.

Jewish tradition and the majority of biblical scholars, archeologists and other researchers think that the first and second temples—Solomon's and Herod's—were located on the "Temple Mount" of Mount Moriah in Jerusalem. Currently on that mount, sit the Dome of the Rock, on the north, and the Al-Aqsa Mosque, on the south.

There are some other scholars, archeologists and researchers who believe that those temples were located in the City of David, right south of the present-day Jerusalem.

Interestingly, historians and archeologists believe there is sufficient evidence to show that this City of David was the site of the original settlement core of both Bronze- and Iron-Age Jerusalem. The Bronze Age, of course, was characterized by the use of bronze, some proto-writing and other features of urban civilization, and went from approximately 3000 B.C. to 1200 B.C. in this region of the world. Included within this timeframe were the Early, Middle and Late Bronze Ages. Some archeologists say that in the area of Britain, the age began as early as 4000 B. C.

The Iron Age in the Near Eastern area began in approximately 1200 B. C. The production of both bronze and iron continued concurrently after that time.

The primary reason for settlements and thereafter, cities, to be located there was the existence of the Gihon Spring, in the Kidron Valley. This was the main source of water for the Pool of Siloam in the City of David.

There have been three different main systems used to have water brought from the Gihon Spring, underground, for use in the current-day Old Jerusalem. Those systems included natural, masonry-built and rock-cut structures.

King David left Hebron and conquered the Jebusite fortress of a small hilltop city, then known as Jerusalem, and established it as the unified capital of the tribes of Israel. The Jebusites were a Canaanite tribe that inhabited that early Jerusalem, whose defeat was first begun by Joshua and completed by David. Apparently, the

Jebusites were of identical ancestry with the Hittites, but got their name from the city of Jebus, which they inhabited, and which later became known as Jerusalem.

POSSIBLE SITES

I will not say which of the two possible sites—Mount Moriah or the City of David—is where the two prior temples were located. Wherever they were, is where the third temple should be built. I cannot argue with the majority who believe it will be on Mount Moriah.

If it needs to be built on Mount Moriah, the Lord could use one or more earthquakes to clear the space needed, and construction could proceed. That quake could also start the flow of water that would heal the Dead Sea.

There is another interesting possibility. In the Salt Lake Valley in Utah, four temples currently stand, and another has been announced to be built there. Two of the current four are located within the city limits of South Jordan, a suburb of Salt Lake City.

Located nearly on the opposite side of modern-day Jerusalem from the City of David is the current Jerusalem Center For Middle Eastern Studies of The Church of Jesus Christ of Latter-day Saints. This center is used for two principal purposes: as housing and classrooms for BYU Studies abroad—in Israel—and for cultural and entertainment events sponsored by the Church, which are open to all citizens of Jerusalem and Israel as a whole.

There is always a possibility that this center could at some time be converted into an additional, second, temple, should the need be determined to exist to allow completion of all of the ordinances that will be necessary for the millions of returning people. There is no revelation claimed here, only a possibility.

BUILDING THE TEMPLE

We know that the lost ten tribes shall return to the land of Israel. As already quoted herein from Jeremiah, they, in "... a great company shall return hither."[126]

And further from the same chapter, they ... "shall sing in the height of Zion."[127] Remember, Mount Zion is in the City of David.

Remember also, Joseph Smith's declaration, already quoted herein:

> Judah must return, Jerusalem must be rebuilt, and the temple, and water come out from under the temple, and the waters of the Dead Sea be healed. It will take some time to rebuild the walls of the city and the temple, etc., and all this must be done before the Son of Man will make His appearance.[128]

We will also re-quote from The Doctrine and Covenants, Section 133, where we are told that the lost ten tribes will return from the north countries, and their enemies shall fall before them.

> And they who are in the north countries shall come in remembrance before the Lord; and their prophets shall hear his voice, and shall no longer stay themselves; and they shall smite the rocks, and the ice shall flow down at their presence.
> And an highway shall be cast up in the midst of the great deep.
> Their enemies shall become a prey unto them,[129]

There is the potential that this third temple in Old Jerusalem, with tens, even hundreds, of thousands of workers from the ten—even twelve—tribes, could be built in a drastically shortened time, after the second major appearance of the Savior's Second Coming—on the Mount of Olives. At that same time, perhaps with multiple earthquakes and other consequences of the return of those lost tribes, those in Israel who would have opposed the construction of this temple, would have been destroyed and the building could proceed unhindered.

As we have read, with the massive earthquake occurring when the Savior stands on the Mount of Olives, only some 200 meters (656 feet) from the wall of Jerusalem on the Temple Mount, the current buildings in the place where the third temple should be built—the Dome of the Rock and Al Aqsa Mosque—could easily be flattened, leaving only rubble and debris to be cleared out of the way.

What about all of the people, nations and armies who would always bring war—jihad—against Israel if it touched the Dome of the Rock or attempted to replace it with a temple? All of those nations and their armies will have been totally defeated, and the wicked destroyed at the end of Armageddon. So, there will be no one to do anything about Israel clearing out the rubble and proceeding to construct the temple in its original place.

Moreover, two other effects of that same earthquake could certainly be the opening up of one or more underground—possibly even very deep underground—aquifers. Whether under the Temple Mount, or in the City of David, that could cause water to come out from under the temple. There could also be sufficient water come to flow to, and heal the Dead Sea.

Plus, there could be a period of many months available between His second major appearance, on the Mount of Olives, and His third appearance, when He comes with power and great glory for all the world to see. That period of time could well be used for that temple's construction.

Chapter 18

BUILDING THE TEMPLE IN NEW JERUSALEM

Elder Spencer W. Kimball spoke of his vision of the construction and beauty of the temple to be built in New Jerusalem—at Independence, Missouri. Speaking to Lamanite people, who are of the seed of Joseph, he said:

> Together you and we shall build in the spectacular city of New Jerusalem the temple to which our Redeemer will come. Your hands with ours, also those of Jacob, will place the foundation stones, raise the walls, and roof of the magnificent structure. Perhaps your artistic hands will paint the temple and decorate it with a master's touch, and together we shall dedicate to our Creator Lord the most beautiful of all temples ever built in his name.[130]

Note, only Ephraim will hold the keys to the ordinances of the temple. But all of the righteous among the House of Israel may have the opportunity to participate in the building of that New Jerusalem Temple.

RETURN OF THE LOST TEN TRIBES

The Doctrine and Covenants provides great insight concerning the time and events at the time of the building of the temple at New Jerusalem.

> 18 When the Lamb shall stand upon Mount Zion, and with him a hundred and forty-four thousand, having his Father's name written on their foreheads.
>
> 20 For behold, he shall stand upon the mount of Olivet, and upon the mighty ocean, even the great deep, and upon the islands of the sea, and upon the land of Zion.
>
> 21 And he shall utter his voice out of Zion, and he shall speak from Jerusalem, and his voice shall be heard among all people;
>
> 24 And the land of Jerusalem and the land of Zion shall be turned back into their own place, and the earth shall be like as it was in the days before it was divided.
>
> 25 And the Lord, even the Savior, shall stand in the midst of his people, and shall reign over all flesh.
>
> 26 And they who are in the north countries shall come in remembrance before the Lord; and their prophets shall hear his voice, and shall no longer stay themselves; and they shall smite the rocks, and the ice shall flow down at their presence.
>
> 27 And an highway shall be cast up in the midst of the great deep.
>
> 28 Their enemies shall become a prey unto them,
>
> 29 And in the barren deserts there shall come forth pools of living water; and the parched ground shall no longer be a thirsty land.
>
> 30 And they shall bring forth their rich treasures unto the children of Ephraim, my servants.
>
> 31 And the boundaries of the everlasting hills shall tremble at their presence.

> 32 And there shall they fall down and be crowned with glory, even in Zion, by the hands of the servants of the Lord, even the children of Ephraim.
>
> 34 Behold, this is the blessing of the everlasting God upon the tribes of Israel, and the richer blessing upon the head of Ephraim and his fellows.[131]

In addition to the lost ten tribes coming to Old Jerusalem, if "the boundaries of the everlasting hills shall tremble at their presence," the ten tribes could also come to the New Jerusalem, in Zion, in Missouri.

Add Elder Kimball's vision. He spoke to the seed of Joseph. He said they and we—members of The Church, <u>and</u> "also those of Jacob" will build the New Jerusalem Temple. Those others of Jacob could include other tribes of Israel. If the ten tribes' "presence" is in the U.S., it would be quite apparent that they would be those others.

Since the lost ten tribes will ultimately return to Old Jerusalem—which satisfies the meaning of "return", the everlasting hills could shake, solely from the earthquake caused by the smashing into, the earth of their "orb." If that orb connects into the polar region, that is, in fact, at the top—the north end—of the everlasting hills, causing the earthquake as prophesied. Then, the ten tribes could simply proceed to Old Jerusalem. So, the possibility is that they may, or may not, go to the New Jerusalem.

We gain further insight into the time frame and the end of the time of the Gentiles, shortly before the Second Coming of the Lord from the following quotation from an address by Elder Wilford Woodruff, delivered in the Tabernacle, in Great Salt Lake City, on February 24, 1855.

> When the Gentiles reject the Gospel **it will be taken from them, and go to the House of Israel**, to that long-suffering people that are now scattered abroad through all the nations upon the earth, . . . and they will rebuild Jerusalem their ancient city, and make

it more glorious than at the beginning, and they will have a leader in Israel with them, a man that is full of the power of God and the gift of the Holy Ghost; but they are held now from this work, only because the *fulness of the Gentiles has not yet come in.*[132]
(Italics added.)

Chapter 19

CONCLUSION

In this book, we have covered a great deal of time, from millennia before the birth of Jesus Christ, until some years beyond the current year, 2020.

We have reviewed the division of the twelve tribes of Israel into two separate kingdoms. Then we focused on the defeat of, first, the northern kingdom—Israel—and then the southern kingdom—Judah. Following the defeat of each kingdom, most of their inhabitants were taken captive, scattered, and—as to the ten tribes—cast out.

Through the years since 586 B. C., when Judah was conquered and removed from Jerusalem, the Jewish people have been almost continually fought against, generally defeated, and scattered among the nations of the earth.

We reviewed the Allegory of the Tame and Wild Olive Trees that prophetically told the story of the history and future of the twelve tribes of Israel.

We saw that the Lord will remember Israel. We next looked at the beginning of the gathering of Israel.

We reviewed the other part of the House of Israel—the seed of Joseph—that is part of the gathering of Israel. We see that God once again continues to fight Israel's battles. Two witnesses—prophets—will fight for Israel. We considered the City of Enoch, and when and to where it will return to the earth.

Next, we examined scripturally and prophetically where the lost ten tribes were taken. We had a good glimpse of the answer in our earlier review of the Allegory of the Tame and Wild Olive Trees. Then we read of the Restoration, or Return, of the Lost Ten Tribes.

Because we have been given some, but not all of the information about the wars and plagues, the destruction of the wicked and the building of the temple in Old Jerusalem, we present that which we know, and consider possible scenarios for that about which we have not been told.

We reviewed the purposes and functions of temples in the Father's eternal plan of redemption and happiness.

Finally, we discussed the building of the temple in Zion, the New Jerusalem, including who will participate.

These important and amazing events will soon come to their completion. Hopefully, we will be spiritually ready to witness and play a positive role in them.

ABOUT THE AUTHOR

Glen W. Park and his wife, Dianne, have six children who are all married. They currently have thirty-four grandchildren.

He is a businessman and attorney. He earned his Bachelor of Arts degree in economics from the University of Utah and a Juris Doctorate from the University of Utah College of Law. He has had executive involvement in a number of successful small businesses. In addition, he has practiced law for more than forty-four years.

He has completed eleven additional books. Nine have already been published. One more is awaiting cover completion. Two additional books are currently in the process of completion.

Included in published books from this author, available at amazon.com and elsewhere, are: 1 - *The Second Coming and The Last Days*; 2 - *Our Next Life: A View Into The Spirit World*; 3 - *What Satan Doesn't Want You To Know*; 4 - *Changing In God's Way*; 5 - *More Than 300 Names, Title & Descriptions of Jesus Christ*; 5 - *Inspiration From The Unknown(s)*; and 6 - *Borrowed Heart: The True Story*.

SOURCES CITED

[1] Jewishvirtuallibrary.org/the-ten-tribes, a project of AICE.
[2] 1 Kings 11:26–35.
[3] 1 Kings 12:19–24.
[4] Isaiah 7:8–9.
[5] Isaiah 8:4.
[6] Jeremiah 3:12.
[7] 1 Kings 14:15-16.
[8] 2 Kings 17:5–8.
[9] 2 Kings 17:18–20.
[10] 2 Kings 18:9–12.
[11] Isaiah 42:24–25.
[12] Isaiah 49:11–12.
[13] Jeremiah 29:1–10.
[14] Jeremiah 29:11–13.
[15] Jeremiah 29:14–20.
[16] Jacob 5:3.
[17] Jacob 5:6–7.
[18] Jacob 5:8.
[19] Jacob 5:14.
[20] Jacob 5:21.
[21] Jacob 5:23.
[22] Jacob 5:25.
[23] Jacob 5:29.
[24] Jacob 5:36.
[25] Jacob 5:48.
[26] Jacob 5:54-56.
[27] Jacob 5:58–59.
[28] Jacob 5:61.
[29] Jacob 5:63, 68.
[30] Jacob 5:75.
[31] Jacob 5:77.
[32] 2 Nephi 10:22.

33 The Doctrine and Covenants 110:11
34 *Documentary History of the Church*, Vol. 4, pp. 456–57.
35 Zechariah 2:12.
36 Zechariah 12:6.
37 3 Nephi 20: 30–31.
38 Isaiah 2:2–3.
39 *Improvement Era,* vol. 22 [1919], pp. 815–16.
40 Jeremiah 16:10–12.
41 Jeremiah 16:13–16.
42 *The Doctrine and Covenants* 110:11.
43 *Pearl of Great Price*; Articles of Faith 1:10.
44 1 Nephi 22:3–9.
45 The Doctrine and Covenants 110: 11.
46 Cowley, pp.509-10.
47 Zechariah 12:6–9
48 Abba Eban, An Autobiography, (N.Y.: Random House, 1977), pp. 400-401.
49 Ibid.
50 2 Nephi 29:11–14.
51 3 Nephi 15:12, 14–23.
52 3 Nephi 17:4.
53 Genesis 49:22.
54 3 Nephi 21:22–26.
55 Ether 13:1-11.
56 Micah 4:10.
57 Micah 4:11-13.
58 Exodus 14:14.
59 Zechariah 14:3, 9.
60 The Doctrine and Covenants 133:41–42.
61 Wilford Woodruff, Experiences in Arizona, pp. 509–10.
62 Zechariah 14:1–3.
63 Zechariah 14:4–9.
64 Zechariah 14:10–21.
65 The Doctrine and Covenants 45:28, 30-33, 35-53, 55–59.
66 The Doctrine and Covenants 77:15, Q and A.
67 Revelation 11:3-13.
68 Conference Report, Orson F. Whitney, October 1919.
69 Journal of Discourses, Orson Pratt, Vol. 2:21.

70 Moses 7:16–21.
71 The Doctrine and Covenants 38:4.
72 The Doctrine and Covenants 45:11–12.
73 The Doctrine and Covenants 84:99–100.
74 Moses 7:62–63.
75 3 Nephi 17:4.
76 Eliza R. Snow, Sacred hymns and Spiritual Songs, 12th Edition, printed by George Tesdale, Liverpool, Hymn 322. (The first edition was published by Brigham Young, P. P. Pratt and John Taylor at Manchester, 1840).
77 Mark E. Petersen, Conference Report, April 1953, Afternoon Meeting, p. 83.
78 The Doctrine and Covenants 133:23-27.
79 The Doctrine and Covenants 133:28-34.
80 HISTORY OF THE CHURCH, Vol. 1:176.
81 Journal of Wilford Woodruff.
82 Questions-By Joseph Fielding and Answers By the Editor (Parley P. Pratt), The Latter-day Saints Millennial Star, Vol. 1 No. 10, February 1841.
83 Jacob Gates Journal, 1881 March, Church History Library, The Church of Jesus Christ of Latter-day Saints.
84 Ibid.
85 Jeremiah 3:18.
86 Jeremiah 16:14–21.
87 Jeremiah 31:7–12.
88 Isaiah 2:3.
89 Josephus, Flavius, *Antiquities of the Jews,* 11:133.
90 Parley P. Pratt, A Voice of Warning, p. 33.
91 Ibid.
92 3 Nephi 17:4.
93 Revelation 9:2–3 and 7-11.
94 Revelation 9:14–21.
95 Zechariah 14:12.
96 The Doctrine and Covenants 61:14–15.
97 Revelation 16:17–20.
98 The Doctrine and Covenants 133:18-23.
99 Revelation 16:21.
100 Micah 5:8, and 3 Nephi 20:16.
101 3 Nephi 8: Heading, and verses 5-19.

[102] 3 Nephi 9:10–14.
[103] Matthew 24:35–41.
[104] Revelation 16:18–21.
[105] Ibid, at No. 76.
[106] Journal of Wilford Woodruff.
[107] Questions-By Joseph Fielding and Answers By the Editor (Parley P. Pratt), The Latter-day Saints Millennial Star, Vol. 1 No. 10, February 1841.
[108] Ibid.
[109] The Doctrine and Covenants Section 133:28.
[110] Malachi 4:5-6.
[111] I Kings 17:1.
[112] ! Kings 17:12-16.
[113] 1 Kings 17:24.
[114] I Kings 18:18-19.
[115] I Kings 18:38-40.
[116] The Doctrine and Covenants 110:13-15.
[117] Micah 4:1-2.
[118] Micah 4:3–5.
[119] Documentary History of the Church, Vol. 5, p. 337.
[120] Micah 4:10.
[121] Zechariah 8:8-9.
[122] The Doctrine and Covenants 124:36-37.
[123] *Newsletter Number 7* of the American Schools of Oriental Research, November 13, 1967.
[124] Ibid.
[125] *Journal of Discourses, V*ol. 19, p. 20.
[126] Jeremiah 31:8 (end of).
[127] Jeremiah 31:12.
[128] Joseph Smith, Documentary History of the Church, Vol. 5, p. 337.
[129] The Doctrine and Covenants 133:26–28.
[130] Spencer W. Kimball, Improvement Era, Dec 1959, pp. 938-39.
[131] The Doctrine and Covenants 133:18, 20-21, 24–32, 34.
[132] Wilford Woodruff, "The Church and Kingdom of God, and the Churches and Kingdoms of Men," delivered on February 24, 1855, *Journal of Discourses,* Volume. 2, p. 200.

www.ingramcontent.com/pod-product-compliance
Lightning Source LLC
Chambersburg PA
CBHW070702100426
42735CB00039B/2497